LONDON
RESTAURANT
GUIDE 2019

RESTAURANTS, BARS & CAFES

The Most Positively
Reviewed and Recommended
Restaurants in the City

EGP
Editorial

LONDON RESTAURANT GUIDE 2019
Restaurants, Gastropubs, Bars & Cafes

© Ronald F. Kinnoch, 2019
© E.G.P. Editorial, 2019

Printed in USA.

ISBN-13: 978-1985768956
ISBN-10: 198576895X

LONDON RESTAURANT GUIDE 2019

Restaurants, Gastropubs, Pubs, Bars & Cafes

*This directory is dedicated to London Business Owners and Managers
who provide the experience that the locals and tourists enjoy.
Thanks you very much for all that you do and thank for being the "People Choice".*

*Thanks to everyone that posts their reviews online and
the amazing reviews sites that make our life easier.*

*The places listed in this book are the most positively reviewed
and recommended by locals and travelers from around the world.*

*Thank you for your time and enjoy the directory that is
designed with locals and tourist in mind!*

TOP 1000
RESTAURANTS

The Most Recommended
(from #1 to #1000)

#1
Regency Café
Cuisines: Coffee & Tea,
Breakfast & Brunch, British
Average price: Under £10
Area: Westminster
Address: 17-19 Regency Street
London SW1P 4BY
Phone: +44 20 7821 6596

#2
The Ledbury
Cuisines: European
Average price: Above £46
Area: Notting Hill
Address: 127 Ledbury Road
London W11 2AQ
Phone: +44 20 7792 9090

#3
Gordon Ramsay
Cuisines: French, Scottish
Average price: Above £46
Area: Chelsea
Address: 69 Royal Hospital Road
London SW3 4HP
Phone: +44 20 7352 4441

#4
Franco Manca
Cuisines: Italian, Pizza
Average price: Under £10
Area: Coldharbour Lane/ Herne Hill
Address: 4 Market Row
London SW9 8LD
Phone: +44 20 7738 3021

#5
Barrafina
Cuisines: Spanish
Average price: £26-45
Area: Soho
Address: 54 Frith Street
London W1D 4SL
Phone: +44 20 7813 8016

#6
The Harp
Cuisines: British, Pub
Average price: £11-25
Area: Covent Garden, Strand
Address: 47 Chandos Place
London WC2N 4HS
Phone: +44 20 7836 0291

#7
Dinner by Heston Blumenthal
Cuisines: British
Average price: Above £46
Area: Hyde Park
Address: 66 Knightsbridge
London SW1X 7LA
Phone: +44 20 7201 3833

#8
Zucca
Cuisines: Italian, Gluten-Free
Average price: £11-25
Area: Borough
Address: 184 Bermondsey Street
London SE1 3TQ
Phone: +44 20 7378 6809

#9
Tiroler Hut
Cuisines: German, Austrian, Fondue
Average price: £11-25
Area: Bayswater
Address: 27 Westbourne Grove
London W2 4UA
Phone: +44 20 7727 3981

#10
Scooter Caffè
Cuisines: Bar, Cafe
Average price: Under £10
Area: Southwark, Waterloo
Address: 132 Lower Marsh
London SE1 7AE
Phone: +44 20 7620 1421

#11
La Fromagerie
Cuisines: Cheese Shop, Deli
Average price: £26-45
Area: Marylebone
Address: 2-6 Moxon Street
London W1U 4EW
Phone: +44 20 7935 0341

#12
Rules Restaurant
Cuisines: British, Bar
Average price: £26-45
Area: Covent Garden, Strand
Address: 35 Maiden Lane
London WC2E 7LB
Phone: +44 20 7836 5314

#13
Big Apple Hot Dogs
Cuisines: Hot Dogs
Average price: £11-25
Area: Camden Town
Address: 34B Camden Lock Place
London NW1 8AL
Phone: +44 20 3592 5526

#14
Petrus Restaurant
Cuisines: French
Average price: Above £46
Area: Belgravia
Address: 1 Kinnerton Street
London SW1X 8EA
Phone: +44 20 7592 1609

#15
Hawksmoor Seven Dials
Cuisines: British, Steakhouse
Average price: £26-45
Area: Covent Garden
Address: 11 Langley Street
London WC2H 9JG
Phone: +44 20 7420 9390

#16
St John Bar and Restaurant
Cuisines: British, Bar
Average price: £26-45
Area: Farringdon
Address: 26 St John Street
London EC1M 4AY
Phone: +44 20 7251 0848

#17
Roundhouse
Cuisines: Music Venues, Performing Arts,
Restaurant, Cultural Center
Average price: £11-25
Area: Camden Town, Chalk Farm
Address: Chalk Farm Road
London NW1 8EH
Phone: +44 844 482 8008

#18
Dishoom Cuisines:
Indian **Average price:**
£11-25
Area: Covent Garden
Address: 12 Upper Saint Martin's Lane
London WC2H 9FB
Phone: +44 20 7420 9320

#19
Homeslice Pizza
Cuisines: Pizza
Average price: £11-25
Area: Covent Garden
Address: 13 Neal's Yard
London WC2H 9DP
Phone: +44 20 7836 4604

#20
Home House
Cuisines: Hotel, Dance Club, British
Average price: £26-45
Area: Marylebone
Address: 20 Portman Square
London W1H 6LW
Phone: +44 20 7670 2000

#21
Le Gavroche
Cuisines: French
Average price: Above £46
Area: Marylebone
Address: 43 Upper Brook Street
London W1K 7QR
Phone: +44 20 7408 0881

#22
La Fromagerie
Cuisines: Deli, Cheese Shop
Average price: £26-45
Area: Highbury
Address: 30 Highbury Park
London N5 2AA
Phone: +44 20 7359 7440

#23
Zuma Restaurant
Cuisines: Japanese, Lounge
Average price: Above £46
Area: Knightsbridge
Address: 5 Raphael Street
London SW7 1DL
Phone: +44 20 7584 1010

#24
Fernandez & Wells
Cuisines: Sandwiches, Cafe
Average price: Under £10
Area: Soho
Address: 73 Beak Street
London W1F 9RS
Phone: +44 20 7287 2814

#25
Swan
Cuisines: British
Average price: £11-25
Area: South Bank, Southwark
Address: 21 New Globe Walk
London SE1 9DT
Phone: +44 20 7928 9444

#26
Great Queen Street
Cuisines: British
Average price: £11-25
Area: Covent Garden
Address: 32 Great Queen Street
London WC2B 5AA
Phone: +44 20 7242 0622

#27
Buen Ayre
Cuisines: Argentine, Steakhouse
Average price: £11-25
Area: Broadway Market,
London Fields
Address: 50 Broadway Market
London E8 4QJ
Phone: +44 20 7275 9900

#28
Amaya
Cuisines: Indian
Average price: Above £46
Area: Belgravia
Address: Halkin Arcade
London SW1X 8LB
Phone: +44 20 7823 1166

#29
Kerbisher & Malt
Cuisines: Fish & Chips
Average price: £11-25
Area: West Kensington
Address: 164 Shepherds Bush Road
London W6 7PB
Phone: +44 20 3556 0228

#30
NOPI
Cuisines: Mediterranean
Average price: £26-45
Area: Soho
Address: 21-22 Warwick Street
London W1B 5NE
Phone: +44 20 7494 9584

#31
Goodman
Cuisines: Steakhouse, Burgers, British
Average price: Above £46
Area: Marylebone
Address: 26 Maddox Street
London W1S 1QH
Phone: +44 20 7499 3776

#32
Honest Burgers
Cuisines: Burgers
Average price: £11-25
Area: Soho
Address: 4A Meard Street
London W1F 0EF
Phone: +44 20 3609 9524

#33
Lucky Voice Karaoke
Cuisines: Karaoke, Bar, Pizza
Average price: £11-25
Area: Islington
Address: 173-174 Upper Street
London N1 1RG
Phone: +44 20 7354 6280

#34
La Crêperie de Hampstead
Cuisines: Creperie, Food Stands
Average price: Under £10
Area: Hampstead Village
Address: 77 Hampstead High Street
London NW3 1RE
Phone: +44 20 7445 6767

#35
Otto
Cuisines: Pizza, Gluten-Free, American
Average price: £11-25
Area: Bayswater, Notting Hill
Address: 6 Chepstow Road
London W2 5BH
Phone: +44 20 7792 4088

#36
Kappacasein
Cuisines: Food Stands, Sandwiches
Average price: Under £10
Area: London Bridge
Address: Stoney Street
London SE1 1TL

#37
Ottolenghi
Cuisines: Mediterranean, European
Average price: £11-25
Area: Islington
Address: 287 Upper Street
London N1 2TZ
Phone: +44 20 7288 1454

#38
Bocca Di Lupo
Cuisines: Italian
Average price: £26-45
Area: Soho
Address: 12 Archer Street
London W1D 7BB
Phone: +44 20 7734 2223

#39
Cafe Du Marche
Cuisines: French
Average price: £26-45
Area: Farringdon
Address: 22 Charterhouse Square
London EC1M 6AH
Phone: +44 20 7608 1609

#40
Workshop Coffee
Cuisines: Coffee & Tea, Cafe
Average price: £11-25
Area: Farringdon
Address: 27 Clerkenwell Road
London EC1M 5RN
Phone: +44 20 7253 5754

#41
Le Relais de Venise L'Entrecôte
Cuisines: French, Steakhouse
Average price: £26-45
Area: Marylebone
Address: 120 Marylebone Lane
London W1U 2QG
Phone: +44 20 7486 0878

#42
Scott's
Cuisines: Seafood, British
Average price: Above £46
Area: Mayfair
Address: 20 Mount Street
London W1K 2HE
Phone: +44 20 7495 7309

#43
Pollen Street Social
Cuisines: British
Average price: Above £46
Area: Marylebone
Address: 8-10 Pollen Street
London W1S 1NQ
Phone: +44 20 7290 7600

#44
Patara
Cuisines: Thai
Average price: £26-45
Area: Bloomsbury
Address: 15 Greek Street
London W1D 4DP
Phone: +44 20 7437 1071

#45
Krispy Kreme Doughnuts
Cuisines: Bakery, Fast Food
Average price: Under £10
Area: Victoria
Address: Victoria station adjacent to
platform 7, London SW1V 1JU

#46
The Wolseley
Cuisines: Cafe, British, Deli
Average price: £26-45
Area: Mayfair
Address: 160 Picadilly
London W1J 9EB
Phone: +44 20 7499 6996

#47
Pied à Terre
Cuisines: French, European, Vegetarian
Average price: Above £46
Area: Fitzrovia
Address: 34 Charlotte Street
London W1T 2NH
Phone: +44 20 7636 1178

#48
Toff's of Muswell Hill
Cuisines: Fish & Chips, British
Average price: £11-25
Area: Muswell Hill
Address: 38 Muswell Hill Broadway
London N10 3RT
Phone: +44 20 8883 8656

#49
Yauatcha
Cuisines: Desserts, Dim Sum, Bakery
Average price: £26-45
Area: Soho
Address: 15-17 Broadwick Street
London W1F 0DL
Phone: +44 20 7494 8888

#50
Pilpel
Cuisines: Middle Eastern, Vegetarian
Average price: Under £10
Area: Aldgate
Address: 38 Brushfield Street
London E1 6AT
Phone: +44 20 7247 0146

#51
Hawksmoor Spitalfields
Cuisines: Steakhouse, British
Average price: £26-45
Area: Spitalfields
Address: 157a Commercial Street
London E1 6BJ
Phone: +44 20 7426 4850

#52
The Harwood Arms
Cuisines: Gastropub, British
Average price: £26-45
Area: West Brompton
Address: 27 Walham Grove
London SW6 1QP
Phone: +44 20 7386 1847

#53
The Berkeley
Cuisines: Hotel, European, Bar
Average price: Above £46
Area: Belgravia
Address: Wilton Place
London SW1X 7RL
Phone: +44 20 7235 6000

#54
Patty & Bun
Cuisines: Burgers
Average price: £11-25
Area: Marylebone
Address: 54 James Street
London W1U 1HE
Phone: +44 20 7487 3188

#55
Taylor St Baristas
Cuisines: Coffee & Tea, Cafe
Average price: £11-25
Area: Aldgate
Address: 1A New Street
London EC2M 4TP
Phone: +44 20 7929 2207

#56
E Pellicci
Cuisines: Italian, Cafe
Average price: Under £10
Area: Shoreditch, Bethnal Green
Address: 332 Bethnal Green Road
London E2 0AG
Phone: +44 20 7739 4873

#57
Food For Thought
Cuisines: Vegetarian
Average price: Under £10
Area: Covent Garden
Address: 31 Neal Street
London WC2H 9PR
Phone: +44 20 7836 0239

#58
Chez Bruce
Cuisines: French
Average price: Above £46
Area: Balham, Wandsworth Common
Address: 2 Bellevue Road
London SW17 7EG
Phone: +44 20 8672 0114

#59
Asakusa
Cuisines: Japanese
Average price: £11-25
Area: Euston, Camden Town
Address: 265 Eversholt Street
London NW1 1BA
Phone: +44 20 7388 8533

#60
L'Atelier de Joël Robuchon
Cuisines: French
Average price: Above £46
Area: Covent Garden
Address: 13-15 West Street
London WC2H 9NE
Phone: +44 20 7010 8600

#61
Burger & Lobster
Cuisines: Seafood, Burgers
Average price: £26-45
Area: Soho
Address: 36 Dean Street
London W1D 4PS
Phone: +44 20 7409 1699

#62
Portland Café
Cuisines: Salad, Cafe, Fast Food
Average price: Under £10
Area: Fitzrovia
Address: 132 Great Portland Street
London W1W 6PU
Phone: +44 20 7580 7510

#63
Railroad
Cuisines: Coffee & Tea, Breakfast &
Brunch, Mediterranean
Average price: Under £10
Area: Homerton
Address: 120-122 Morning Lane
London E9 6LH
Phone: +44 20 8985 2858

#64
Ye Olde Cheshire Cheese
Cuisines: Pub, British
Average price: £11-25
Area: Blackfriars, Holborn
Address: 145 Fleet Street
London EC4A 2BU
Phone: +44 20 7353 6170

#65
Sketch
Cuisines: French, Venues,
Event Space, European
Average price: £26-45
Area: Marylebone, Piccadilly
Address: 9 Conduit Street
London W1S 2XG
Phone: +44 20 7659 4500

#66
Luna Nuova
Cuisines: Italian
Average price: £11-25
Area: Fulham
Address: 773 Fulham Road
London SW6 5HA
Phone: +44 20 7371 9774

#67
Freebird Burritos
Cuisines: Mexican, Food Stands
Average price: Under £10
Area: Soho
Address: London W1F 0RG

#68
Roti Chai
Cuisines: Indian
Average price: £11-25
Area: Marylebone
Address: 3 Portman Mews S
London W1H 6AS
Phone: +44 20 7408 0101

#69
Maggie Jones's
Cuisines: British
Average price: £26-45
Area: Kensington
Address: 6 Old Court Place
London W8 4PL
Phone: +44 20 7937 6462

#70
Alounak
Cuisines: Persian/Iranian
Average price: £11-25
Area: Bayswater
Address: 44 Westbourne Grove
London W2 5SH
Phone: +44 20 7229 0416

#71
Vrisaki Kebab House
Cuisines: Greek
Average price: £11-25
Area: Bowes Park, Wood Green
Address: 73 Myddleton Road
London N22 8LZ
Phone: +44 20 8881 2920

#72
The Connaught
Cuisines: Hotel, European, Bar
Average price: Above £46
Area: Mayfair **Address:**
Carlos Place London
W1K 2AL
Phone: +44 20 7499 7070

#73
Busaba Eathai
Cuisines: Thai
Average price: £11-25
Area: Soho
Address: 106-110 Wardour Street
London W1F 0TR
Phone: +44 20 7255 8686

#74
Bar Italia
Cuisines: Coffee & Tea, Italian, Bar
Average price: £26-45
Area: Bloomsbury
Address: 22 Frith Street
London W1D 4RP
Phone: +44 20 7437 4520

#75
Ozone Coffee
Cuisines: Coffee & Tea,
Breakfast & Brunch
Average price: £11-25
Area: Liverpool Street / Broadgate
Address: 11 Leonard Street
London EC2A 4AQ
Phone: +44 20 7490 1039

#76
Le Mercury
Cuisines: French
Average price: £11-25
Area: Islington
Address: 140a Upper Street
London N1 1QY
Phone: +44 20 7354 4088

#77
Quilon Restaurant
Cuisines: Indian
Average price: £26-45
Area: Westminster
Address: 41 Buckingham Gate
London SW1E 6AF
Phone: +44 20 7821 1899

#78
Addie's Thai Cafe
Cuisines: Thai
Average price: £11-25
Area: South Kensington
Address: 121 Earl's Court Road
London SW5 9RL
Phone: +44 20 7259 2620

#79
Terroirs
Cuisines: Wine Bar, French
Average price: £26-45
Area: Covent Garden, Strand
Address: 5 William IV Street
London WC2N 4DW
Phone: +44 20 7036 0660

#80
Ciao Bella
Cuisines: Italian
Average price: £11-25
Area: Bloomsbury
Address: 86-90 Lambs Conduit Street
London WC1N 3LZ
Phone: +44 20 7242 4119

#81
The Windsor Castle
Cuisines: Pub, British
Average price: £11-25
Area: Kensington
Address: 114 Campden Hill Road
London W8 7AR
Phone: +44 20 7243 8797

#82
The Golden Hind
Cuisines: Fish & Chips
Average price: £11-25
Area: Marylebone
Address: 73 Marylebone Lane
London W1U 2PN
Phone: +44 20 7486 3644

#83
Look Mum No Hands!
Cuisines: Coffee & Tea, Bikes, Cafe
Average price: Under £10
Area: Barbican
Address: 49 Old Street
London EC1V 9HX
Phone: +44 20 7253 1025

#84
Rasoi Vineet Bhatia
Cuisines: Indian
Average price: Above £46
Area: Chelsea
Address: 10 Lincoln Street
London SW3 2TS
Phone: +44 20 7225 1881

#85
The Cinnamon Club
Cuisines: Indian, Pakistani, Cocktail Bar
Average price: Above £46
Area: Westminster
Address: 30-32 Great Smith Street
London SW1P 3BU
Phone: +44 20 7222 2555

#86
Masters Super Fish
Cuisines: Fish & Chips
Average price: Under £10
Area: Southwark
Address: 191 Waterloo Road
London SE1 8UX
Phone: +44 20 7928 6924

#87
José
Cuisines: Spanish, Bar, Tapas Bar
Average price: £11-25
Area: Borough
Address: 104 Bermondsey Street
London SE1 3UB
Phone: +44 20 7403 4902

#88
Maoz
Cuisines: Fast Food, Vegetarian
Average price: Under £10
Area: Soho
Address: 43 Old Compton Street
London W1D 6HG
Phone: +44 20 7851 1586

#89
Milk Bar Cuisines:
Cafe **Average price:**
£11-25
Area: Bloomsbury
Address: 3 Bateman Street
London W1D 4AG
Phone: +44 20 7287 4796

#90
Curious Yellow Kafé
Cuisines: Scandinavian,
Breakfast & Brunch
Average price: Under £10
Area: Hoxton
Address: 77 Pitfield Street
London N1 6BT
Phone: +44 20 7251 6018

#91
Cookies and Scream
Cuisines: Coffee & Tea, Bakery, Vegan
Average price: Under £10
Area: Camden Town
Address: Camden Lock Place
London NW1 8AF
Phone: +44 7778 691519

#92
Upstairs
Cuisines: French, Bar
Average price: £26-45
Area: Brixton
Address: 89b Acre Lane
London SW2 5TN
Phone: +44 20 7733 8855

#93
Donostia
Cuisines: Tapas
Average price: £26-45
Area: Marylebone
Address: 10 Seymour Place
London W1H 7ND
Phone: +44 20 3620 1845

#94
Hakkasan
Cuisines: Chinese
Average price: Above £46
Area: Fitzrovia
Address: 8 Hanway Place
London W1T 1HD
Phone: +44 20 7927 7000

#95
H T Harris
Cuisines: Deli, Coffee & Tea,
Delicatessen, Cafe
Average price: £11-25
Area: Fitzrovia
Address: 41 Great Titchfield Street
London W1W 7PG
Phone: +44 20 7636 4228

#96
Savoir Faire
Cuisines: French
Average price: £11-25
Area: Bloomsbury
Address: 42 New Oxford Street
London WC1A 1EP
Phone: +44 20 7436 0707

#97
Duck & Waffle
Cuisines: European
Average price: £26-45
Area: Aldgate
Address: 110 BiShopgate 40th Floor
London EC2N 4AY
Phone: +44 20 3640 7310

#98
Burger & Lobster
Cuisines: American, Burgers, Seafood
Average price: £11-25
Area: Mayfair
Address: 29 Clarges Street
London W1J 7EF
Phone: +44 20 7409 1699

#99
Galvin Bistrot de Luxe
Cuisines: French
Average price: £26-45
Area: Marylebone
Address: 66 Baker Street
London W1U 7DJ
Phone: +44 20 7935 4007

#100
Ten Ten Tei
Cuisines: Sushi Bar, Japanese
Average price: £11-25
Area: Soho
Address: 56 Brewer Street
London W1F 9TJ
Phone: +44 20 7287 1738

#101
St. Martin-in-the-Fields Church
Cuisines: Cafe, Landmark, Church,
Historical Buildings
Area: Strand
Address: St Martin's Place
London WC2N 4JJ
Phone: +44 20 7766 1100

#102
Koya
Cuisines: Japanese
Average price: £11-25
Area: Soho
Address: 49 Frith Street
London W1D 4SG
Phone: +44 20 7434 4463

#103
Il Portico
Cuisines: Italian
Average price: £26-45
Area: Kensington
Address: 277 Kensington High Street
London W8 6NA
Phone: +44 20 7602 6262

#104
Roast To Go
Cuisines: British, Food Stands
Average price: Under £10
Area: London Bridge
Address: Stoney Street
London SE1 1TL

#105
Chutney Mary
Cuisines: Indian
Average price: Above £46
Area: West Brompton
Address: 535 Kings Road Chelsea
London SW10 0SZ
Phone: +44 20 7351 3113

#106
Ruby
Cuisines: Italian, Sandwiches, Cafe
Average price: Under £10
Area: Liverpool Street / Broadgate
Address: 35 Charlotte Road
London EC2A 3PB

#107
Rasa
Cuisines: Indian, Pakistani
Average price: £11-25
Area: Marylebone
Address: 6 Dering Street
London W1C 1JN
Phone: +44 20 7629 1346

#108
Bailey's Fish and Chips
Cuisines: Fish & Chips
Average price: Under £10
Area: Fulham
Address: 115 Dawes Road
London SW6 7EQ
Phone: +44 20 7385 2021

#109
Ibérica
Cuisines: Wine Bar, Spanish, Tapas
Average price: £26-45
Area: Fitzrovia
Address: 195 Great Portland Street
London W1W 5PS
Phone: +44 20 7636 8650

#110
Honest Burgers
Cuisines: Burgers
Average price: £11-25
Area: Bloomsbury
Address: 251 Pentonville Road
London N1 9NG
Phone: +44 20 3302 3452

#111
Amato's Patisserie
Cuisines: Cafe
Average price: £11-25
Area: Soho
Address: 14 Old Compton Street
London W1D 4TH
Phone: +44 871 527 0515

#112
Rasa Travancore
Cuisines: Indian
Average price: £11-25
Area: Stoke Newington, Stoke Newington Church Street
Address: 56 Stoke Newington Church St
London N16 0AR
Phone: +44 20 7249 1340

#113
Abeno
Cuisines: Japanese
Average price: £11-25
Area: Bloomsbury
Address: 47 Museum Street
London WC1A 1LY
Phone: +44 20 7405 3211

#114
Caravan
Cuisines: Breakfast & Brunch, Coffee & Tea
Average price: £11-25
Area: Clerkenwell
Address: 11-13 Exmouth Market
London EC1R 4QD
Phone: +44 20 7833 8115

#115
Princi
Cuisines: Italian, Bakery, Coffee & Tea
Average price: £11-25
Area: Soho
Address: 135 Wardour Street
London W1F 0UT
Phone: +44 20 7478 8888

#116
Pizzeria Pappagone
Cuisines: Italian
Average price: £11-25
Area: Stroud Green
Address: 131 Stroud Green Road
London N4 3PX
Phone: +44 20 7263 2114

#117
The Churchill Arms
Cuisines: Pub, Thai
Average price: £11-25
Area: Notting Hill
Address: 119 Kensington Church Street
London W8 7LN
Phone: +44 20 7727 4242

#118
Roka
Cuisines: Japanese
Average price: Above £46
Area: Fitzrovia
Address: 37 Charlotte Street
London W1T 1RR
Phone: +44 20 7580 6464

#119
Villa Bianca
Cuisines: Italian
Average price: £11-25
Area: Hampstead Village
Address: 1 Perrins Court
London NW3 1QS
Phone: +44 20 7435 3131

#120
The Old School Yard
Cuisines: Cocktail Bar, Dive Bar, Pizza
Average price: £11-25
Area: Borough
Address: 111 Long Lane
London SE1 4PH
Phone: +44 20 7357 6281

#121
J Sheekey
Cuisines: Seafood
Average price: £26-45
Area: Covent Garden, Strand
Address: 28-34 St Martin's Court
London WC2N 4AL
Phone: +44 20 7240 2565

#122
Goodman City
Cuisines: Steakhouse
Average price: Above £46
Area: The City
Address: 11 Old Jewry
London EC2R 8DU
Phone: +44 20 7600 8220

#123
Tommi's Burger Joint
Cuisines: Burgers
Average price: Under £10
Area: Marylebone
Address: 30 Thayer Street
London W1U 2QP
Phone: +44 20 7224 3828

#124
Launceston Place
Cuisines: British
Average price: Above £46
Area: Kensington
Address: 1A Launceston Place
London W8 5RL
Phone: +44 20 7937 6912

#125
Hot Stuff Cuisines:
Indian **Average price:**
£11-25
Area: South Lambeth
Address: 19 Wilcox Road
London SW8 2XA
Phone: +44 20 7720 1480

#126
Noodle Bar
Cuisines: Chinese
Average price: Under £10
Area: Covent Garden
Address: 33 Cranbourne Street
London WC2H 7AD
Phone: +44 20 7467 4546

#127
KIN
Cuisines: Asian Fusion, Fast Food, Thai
Average price: £11-25
Area: Farringdon
Address: 88 Leather Lane
London EC1N 7TT
Phone: +44 20 7430 0886

#128
The Greenwich Union
Cuisines: British, Pub
Average price: £11-25
Area: Greenwich
Address: 56 Royal Hill
London SE10 8RT
Phone: +44 20 8692 6258

#129
Santa Maria Pizzeria
Cuisines: Pizza
Average price: £11-25
Area: Ealing
Address: 15 St Mary's Road
London W5 5RA
Phone: +44 20 8579 1462

#130
The Veggie Table
Cuisines: Vegetarian
Average price: Under £10
Area: London Bridge
Address: 8 Southwark Street
London SE1 1TL
Phone: +44 20 3417 4542

#131
Zayna
Cuisines: Indian, Pakistani
Average price: £26-45
Area: Marylebone
Address: 25 New Quebec Street
London W1H 7SF
Phone: +44 20 7723 2229

#132
ICCo
Cuisines: Pizza, Italian
Average price: Under £10
Area: Fitzrovia
Address: 46 Goodge Street
London W1T 4LU
Phone: +44 20 7580 9688

#133
The Orange Buffalo
Cuisines: Chicken Wings, Street Vendor,
Fast Food
Average price: Under £10
Area: Brick Lane, Shoreditch
Address: Brick Lane
London E1 6QL
Phone: +44 7925 821229

#134
Santore
Cuisines: Italian
Average price: £11-25
Area: Clerkenwell
Address: 59-61 Exmouth Market
London EC1R 4QL
Phone: +44 20 7812 1488

#135
Selale
Cuisines: Turkish
Average price: Under £10
Area: Harringay, West Green
Address: 1-2 Salisbury Promenade
London N8 0RX
Phone: +44 20 8800 1636

#136
The Table
Cuisines: British, Coffee & Tea, Breakfast
& Brunch
Average price: £11-25
Area: Southwark
Address: 83 Southwark Street
London SE1 0HX
Phone: +44 20 7401 2760

#137
Bottega Prelibato
Cuisines: Coffee & Tea, Italian, Deli
Average price: £11-25
Area: Hoxton
Address: 45 Rivington Street
London EC2A 3QB

#138
Veeraswamy
Cuisines: Indian
Average price: Above £46
Area: Piccadilly
Address: 99 Regent Street
London W1B 4RS
Phone: +44 20 7734 1401

#139
Bistrotheque
Cuisines: French
Average price: £26-45
Area: Bethnal Green
Address: 23-27 Wadeson Street
London E2 9DR
Phone: +44 20 8983 7900

#140
Medcalf
Cuisines: British, Gastropub
Average price: £11-25
Area: Clerkenwell
Address: 40 Exmouth Market
London EC1R 4QE
Phone: +44 20 7833 3533

#141
L'Autre Pied
Cuisines: French, European, Vegetarian
Average price: Above £46
Area: Marylebone
Address: 5-7 Blandford Street
London W1U 3DB
Phone: +44 20 7486 9696

#142
CASK Pub and Kitchen
Cuisines: Pub, Gastropub
Average price: £11-25
Area: Pimlico
Address: 6 Charlwood Street
London SW1V 2EE
Phone: +44 20 7630 7225

#143
Laughing Halibut
Cuisines: Fish & Chips
Average price: Under £10
Area: Westminster
Address: 38 Strutton Ground
London SW1P 2HR
Phone: +44 20 7799 2844

#144
The Pineapple
Cuisines: Pub, Thai, Gastropub
Average price: £11-25
Area: Kentish Town
Address: 51 Leverton Street
London NW5 2NX
Phone: +44 20 7284 4631

#145
Texture
Cuisines: Champagne Bar, European
Average price: £26-45
Area: Marylebone
Address: 34 Portman Street
London W1H 7BY
Phone: +44 20 7224 0028

#146
The Faltering Fullback
Cuisines: Thai, Pub
Average price: £11-25
Area: Finsbury Park, Stroud Green
Address: 19 Perth Road
London N4 3HB
Phone: +44 20 7272 5834

#147
Best Mangal
Cuisines: Turkish, Middle Eastern
Average price: £11-25
Area: West Kensington
Address: 66 North End Road
London W14 9EP
Phone: +44 20 7602 0212

#148
Camisa & Son
Cuisines: Deli
Average price: £11-25
Area: Soho
Address: 61 Old Compton Street
London W1D 6HS
Phone: +44 20 7437 7610

#149
Wahaca Cuisines:
Mexican **Average**
price: £11-25
Area: Soho
Address: 80 Wardour Street
London W1F 0TF
Phone: +44 20 7734 0195

#150
Franco Manca
Cuisines: Italian, Pizza
Average price: Under £10
Area: Chiswick
Address: 144 Chiswick High Rd
London W4 1PU
Phone: +44 20 8747 4822

#151
Mosob Restaurant
Cuisines: African, Ethiopian
Average price: £11-25
Area: Maida Hill
Address: 339 Harrow Road
London W9 3RB
Phone: +44 20 7267 2012

#152
Clos Maggiore
Cuisines: French, Mediterranean
Average price: £26-45
Area: Covent Garden
Address: 33 King Street
London WC2E 8JD
Phone: +44 20 7379 9696

#153
Wahaca
Cuisines: Mexican
Average price: £11-25
Area: Covent Garden, Strand
Address: 66 Chandos Place
London WC2N 4HG
Phone: +44 20 7240 1883

#154
Atari-Ya Sushi Bar
Cuisines: Fast Food, Sushi Bar
Average price: £11-25
Area: Marylebone
Address: 20 James Street
London W1U 1EH
Phone: +44 20 7491 1178

#155
Osteria Basilico
Cuisines: Italian
Average price: £26-45
Area: Notting Hill
Address: 29 Kensington Park Road
London W11 2EU
Phone: +44 20 7727 9957

#156
Golden Union Fish Bar
Cuisines: Fish & Chips
Average price: £11-25
Area: Soho
Address: 38 Poland Street
London W1F 7LY
Phone: +44 20 7434 1933

#157
Hawksmoor Air Street
Cuisines: Seafood, Steakhouse
Average price: Above £46
Area: Piccadilly
Address: 5A Air Street
London W1J 0AD
Phone: +44 20 7406 3980

#158
Gallipoli
Cuisines: Turkish, Bistro, Cafe
Average price: £11-25
Area: Angel, Islington
Address: 102 Upper Street
London N1 1QN
Phone: +44 20 7359 0630

#159
OXO Tower Restaurant
Cuisines: British, Lounge
Average price: £26-45
Area: South Bank, Southwark
Address: Barge House Street
London SE1 9PH
Phone: +44 20 7803 3888

#160
Abeno Too
Cuisines: Japanese
Average price: £11-25
Area: Covent Garden
Address: 17-18 Great Newport Street
London WC2H 7JE
Phone: +44 20 7379 1160

#161
The Counter Cafe
Cuisines: Coffee & Tea,
Breakfast & Brunch
Average price: £11-25
Area: Bow, Stratford
Address: 7 Roach Road
London E3 2PA
Phone: +44 7834 275920

#162
Bodean's
Cuisines: Barbeque, Burgers
Average price: £11-25
Area: Soho
Address: 10a Poland Street
London W1F 8PZ
Phone: +44 20 7287 7575

#163
Ganapati
Cuisines: Indian
Average price: £11-25
Area: Peckham
Address: 38 Holly Grove
London SE15 5DF
Phone: +44 20 7277 2928

#164
Le Sacre Coeur
Cuisines: French
Average price: £11-25
Area: Angel, Islington
Address: 18 Theberton Street
London N1 0QX
Phone: +44 20 7354 2618

#165
Honest Burgers
Cuisines: Burgers
Average price: Under £10
Area: Coldharbour Lane/ Herne Hill
Address: Unit 12 Brixton Market
London SW9 8PR
Phone: +44 20 7733 7963

#166
Kitchen Table
Cuisines: American, European
Average price: Above £46
Area: Fitzrovia
Address: 70 Charlotte Street
London W1T 4QG
Phone: +44 20 7637 7770

#167
Trinity Restaurant
Cuisines: European, British
Average price: Above £46
Area: Clapham
Address: 4 The Polygon
London SW4 0JG
Phone: +44 20 7622 1199

#168
Towpath Café
Cuisines: Mediterranean,
European, Coffee & Tea
Average price: £11-25
Area: De Beauvoir
Address: 42 De Beauvoir Crescent
London N1 5SB
Phone: +44 20 7254 7606

#169
Fernandez & Wells
Cuisines: Coffee & Tea, Sandwiches
Average price: £11-25
Area: Soho
Address: 43 Lexington Street
London W1F 9AL
Phone: +44 20 7734 1546

#170
The Pig and Butcher
Cuisines: British, Gastropub
Average price: £26-45
Area: Angel, Islington
Address: 80 Liverpool Road
London N1 0QD
Phone: +44 20 7226 8304

#171
La Petite Maison
Cuisines: French
Average price: Above £46
Area: Marylebone
Address: 54 Brooks Mews
London W1K 4EG
Phone: +44 20 7495 4774

#172
Hunan
Cuisines: Chinese
Average price: Above £46
Address: 51 Pimlico Road
London SW1W 8NE

#173
Gauthier Soho
Cuisines: French
Average price: Above £46
Area: Bloomsbury
Address: 21 Romilly Street
London W1D 5AF
Phone: +44 20 7494 3111

#174
The Gate
Cuisines: Vegetarian
Average price: £26-45
Area: Hammersmith
Address: 51 Queen Caroline Street
London W6 9QL
Phone: +44 20 8748 6932

#175
Table For 10
Cuisines: Vietnamese
Average price: £26-45
Area: Whitechapel
Address: Whitechappel
London E1 5BB

#176
Misato
Cuisines: Japanese
Average price: Under £10
Area: Leicester Square
Address: 11 Wardour Street
London W1D 6PG
Phone: +44 20 7734 0808

#177
Belgo Centraal
Cuisines: Belgian
Average price: £11-25
Area: Covent Garden
Address: 50 Earlham Street
London WC2H 9LJ
Phone: +44 20 7813 2233

#178
Bob Bob Ricard
Cuisines: British, Russian, Bar
Average price: £26-45
Area: Soho
Address: 1 Upper St James Street
London W1F 9DF
Phone: +44 20 3145 1000

#179
Pitt Cue Co
Cuisines: Bar, American, Barbeque
Average price: £11-25
Area: Soho
Address: 1 Newburgh Street
London W1F 7RB

#180
Maze Grill
Cuisines: Sushi Bar, Steakhouse
Average price: Above £46
Area: Marylebone
Address: 10-13 Grosvenor Square
London W1K 6JP
Phone: +44 20 7107 0000

#181
Nobu Berkeley St
Cuisines: Japanese, Sushi Bar
Average price: Above £46
Area: Mayfair
Address: 15 Berkeley Street
London W1J 8DY
Phone: +44 20 7290 9222

#182
North Sea Fish Restaurant
Cuisines: Seafood, Fish & Chips
Average price: £11-25
Area: Bloomsbury
Address: 7-8 Leigh Street
London WC1H 9EW
Phone: +44 20 7387 5892

#183
Arbutus
Cuisines: British, European
Average price: £26-45
Area: Soho
Address: 63-64 Frith Street
London W1D 3JW
Phone: +44 20 7734 4545

#184
Scandinavian Kitchen
Cuisines: Grocery, Scandinavian,
Ethnic Food
Average price: £11-25
Area: Fitzrovia
Address: 61 Great Titchfield Street
London W1W 7PP
Phone: +44 20 7580 7161

#185
Pret A Manger
Cuisines: Coffee & Tea, Fast Food,
Sandwiches
Average price: £11-25
Area: Piccadilly
Address: 163 Piccadilly
London W1J 9ED
Phone: +44 20 7932 5229

#186
The Orangery
Cuisines: British, Tea Room
Average price: £11-25
Area: Hyde Park, Kensington, Kensington
Gardens
Address: Kensington Palace
London W8 3UY
Phone: +44 20 3166 6113

#187
The Book Club
Cuisines: Music Venues,
Sandwiches, British
Average price: £11-25
Area: Liverpool Street / Broadgate
Address: 100 Leonard Street
London EC2A 4RH
Phone: +44 20 7684 8618

#188
Maroush II
Cuisines: Middle Eastern
Average price: £11-25
Area: Chelsea
Address: 38 Beauchamp Place
London SW3 1NU
Phone: +44 20 7581 5434

#189
Bar Boulud
Cuisines: French
Average price: £26-45
Area: Belgravia, Hyde Park
Address: 66 Knightsbridge
London SW1X 7LA
Phone: +44 20 7201 3899

#190
Galvin at Windows
Cuisines: French
Average price: Above £46
Area: Mayfair
Address: 22 Park Lane
London W1K 1BE
Phone: +44 20 7208 4021

#191
Punjab
Cuisines: Indian
Average price: £11-25
Area: Covent Garden
Address: 80 Neal Street
London WC2H 9PA
Phone: +44 20 7836 9787

#192
Holly Bush
Cuisines: Pub, Gastropub
Average price: £11-25
Area: Hampstead Village
Address: 22 Holly Mount
London NW3 6SG
Phone: +44 20 7435 2892

#193
Four Seasons Hotel
Cuisines: Hotel, Tea Room
Average price: Above £46
Area: Mayfair
Address: Hamilton Place
London W1A 7DR
Phone: +44 20 7499 0888

#194
BLT Deli
Cuisines: Deli
Average price: £11-25
Area: Liverpool Street / Broadgate
Address: 55 Curtain Road
London EC2A 3PT
Phone: +44 20 7613 5322

#195
**The Lanesborough Hotel
Afternoon Tea**
Cuisines: Hotel, Tea Room, European
Average price: Above £46
Area: Hyde Park
Address: Lanesborough Place
London SW1X 7TA
Phone: +44 20 7259 5599

#196
Antepliler
Cuisines: Turkish
Average price: Under £10
Area: Harringay
Address: 46 Grand Parade
London N4 1AG
Phone: +44 20 8802 5588

#197
Rinkoff Bakery
Cuisines: Bakery, Sandwiches
Average price: Under £10
Area: Whitechapel
Address: 224 Jubilee Street
London E1 3BS
Phone: +44 20 7791 4909

#198
Bibimbap Soho
Cuisines: Korean
Average price: Under £10
Area: Bloomsbury
Address: 11 Greek Street
London W1D 4DJ
Phone: +44 20 7287 3434

#199
Mohsen
Cuisines: Persian/Iranian
Average price: £11-25
Area: Kensington
Address: 152 Warwick Road
London W14 8PS
Phone: +44 20 7603 9888

#200
Petek
Cuisines: Turkish
Average price: £11-25
Area: Finsbury Park, Stroud Green
Address: 96 Stroud Green Road
London N4 3EN
Phone: +44 20 7619 3933

#201
Poppies
Cuisines: Fish & Chips, Fast Food
Average price: £11-25
Area: Brick Lane, Shoreditch
Address: 6-8 Hanbury Street
London E1 6QR
Phone: +44 20 7247 0892

#202
L'Anima
Cuisines: Italian, Cafe
Average price: Above £46
Area: Liverpool Street / Broadgate
Address: 1 Snowden Street
London EC2A 2DQ
Phone: +44 20 7422 7000

#203
The Chancery
Cuisines: British
Average price: £26-45
Area: Holborn
Address: 9 Cursitor Street
London EC4A 1LL
Phone: +44 20 7831 4000

#204
Corner Room
Cuisines: European
Average price: £26-45
Area: Bethnal Green
Address: Patriot Square
London E2 9NF
Phone: +44 20 7871 0460

#205
Dotori
Cuisines: Korean, Japanese
Average price: £11-25
Area: Finsbury Park
Address: 3 Stroud Green Road
London N4 2DQ
Phone: +44 20 7263 3562

#206
Jumbo Eats
Cuisines: Sandwiches
Average price: Under £10
Area: Soho
Address: 59 Brewer Street
London W1F 9UN
Phone: +44 20 7494 2133

#207
inSpiral Lounge
Cuisines: Vegetarian, Vegan,
Music Venues
Average price: £11-25
Area: Camden Town
Address: 250 Camden High Street
London NW1 8QS
Phone: +44 872 148 6585

#208
The Ivy
Cuisines: European
Average price: £26-45
Area: Covent Garden
Address: 1 - 5 West Street
London WC2H 9NQ
Phone: +44 20 7836 4751

#209
Kazan
Cuisines: Turkish
Average price: £11-25
Area: Victoria
Address: 93 Wilton Road
London SW1V 1DW
Phone: +44 20 7233 7100

#210
La Porchetta Pollo Bar
Cuisines: Italian
Average price: Under £10
Area: Bloomsbury
Address: 20 Old Compton Street
London W1D 4TW
Phone: +44 20 7494 9368

#211
The English Restaurant
Cuisines: British
Average price: £11-25
Area: Aldgate
Address: 50-52 Brushfield St
London E1 6AG
Phone: +44 20 7247 4110

#212
Malletti
Cuisines: Pizza
Average price: £11-25
Area: Soho
Address: 26 Noel Street
London W1F 8GY
Phone: +44 20 7439 4096

#213
Muffinski's
Cuisines: Bakery, Ice Cream,
Gluten-Free
Average price: Under £10
Area: Covent Garden, Strand
Address: 5 King Street
London WC2E 8HN
Phone: +44 20 7379 1525

#214
Timberyard
Cuisines: Cafe, Coffee & Tea
Average price: £11-25
Area: Barbican
Address: 61-67 Old Street
London EC1V 9HW

#215
**Vasco & Piero's Pavilion
Restaurant**
Cuisines: Italian
Average price: £26-45
Area: Soho
Address: 15 Poland Street
London W1F 8QE
Phone: +44 20 7437 8774

#216
Tibits
Cuisines: Vegetarian
Average price: £11-25
Area: Piccadilly
Address: 12-14 Heddon Street
London W1B 4DA
Phone: +44 20 7745 6146

#217
York & Albany
Cuisines: Hotel, Wine Bar, British
Average price: £26-45
Area: Euston, Camden Town
Address: 127-129 Parkway
London NW1 7PS
Phone: +44 20 7388 3344

#218
Flat Iron
Cuisines: Steakhouse
Average price: £11-25
Area: Soho
Address: 17 Beak Street
London W1F 9RW

#219
Cafe East
Cuisines: Vietnamese
Average price: Under £10
Area: Bermondsey, Canada Water,
Rotherhithe, Surrey Quays
Address: 100 Redriff Road
London SE16 7LH
Phone: +44 20 7252 1212

#220
Seven Stars
Cuisines: Pub, British
Average price: £11-25
Area: Holborn
Address: 53-54 Carey Street
London WC2A 2JB
Phone: +44 20 7242 8521

#221
Marquis Cornwallis
Cuisines: Pub, British
Average price: £11-25
Area: Bloomsbury
Address: 31 Marchmont Street
London WC1N 1AP
Phone: +44 20 7278 8355

#222
Mr Kong
Cuisines: Chinese
Average price: £11-25
Area: Chinatown
Address: 21 Lisle Street
London WC2H 7BA
Phone: +44 20 7437 7341

#223
Kazan
Cuisines: Turkish
Average price: £11-25
Area: Victoria
Address: 93 Wilton Road
London SW1V 1DW
Phone: +44 20 7233 7100

#224
Mildreds
Cuisines: Vegetarian, Vegan
Average price: £11-25
Area: Soho
Address: 45 Lexington Street
London W1F 9AN
Phone: +44 20 7494 1634

#225
Sager + Wilde
Cuisines: Wine Bar, Tapas
Average price: £26-45
Area: Shoreditch, Haggerston
Address: 193 Hackney Road
London E2 8JL

#226
Ottolenghi
Cuisines: Bakery, Mediterranean
Average price: £11-25
Area: Notting Hill
Address: 63 Ledbury Road
London W11 2AD
Phone: +44 20 7727 1121

#227
Pret A Manger
Cuisines: Coffee & Tea, Breakfast &
Brunch, Sandwiches
Average price: Under £10
Area: Marylebone
Address: 381 Oxford Street
London W1C 2JS
Phone: +44 20 7932 5280

#228
The Grenadier
Cuisines: British, Pub
Average price: £11-25
Area: Belgravia
Address: 18 Wilton Row
London SW1X 7NR
Phone: +44 20 7235 3074

#229
Spuntino
Cuisines: Tapas
Average price: £11-25
Area: Soho
Address: 61 Rupert Street
London W1D 7PL

#230
Hakkasan
Cuisines: Chinese
Average price: Above £46
Area: Mayfair
Address: 17 Bruton Street
London W1J 6QB
Phone: +44 20 7907 1888

#231
Yalla Yalla
Cuisines: Middle Eastern
Average price: £11-25
Area: Soho
Address: 1 Green's Court
London W1F 0HA
Phone: +44 20 7287 7663

#232
Gaucho
Cuisines: Steakhouse, Argentine
Average price: Above £46
Area: Fitzrovia
Address: 60A Charlotte Street
London W1T 2NU
Phone: +44 20 7580 6252

#233
Salt Yard
Cuisines: Tapas Bar, Wine Bar
Average price: £26-45
Area: Fitzrovia
Address: 54 Goodge Street
London W1T 4NA
Phone: +44 20 7637 0657

#234
Tsunami
Cuisines: Japanese
Average price: £26-45
Area: Fitzrovia
Address: 93 Charlotte Street
London W1T 4PY
Phone: +44 20 7637 0050

#235
Cambio De Tercio
Cuisines: Spanish
Average price: £26-45
Area: South Kensington
Address: 163 Old Brompton Road
London SW5 0LJ
Phone: +44 20 7244 8970

#236
Reubens
Cuisines: Kosher, Deli
Average price: £11-25
Area: Marylebone
Address: 79 Baker Street
London W1U 6AG
Phone: +44 20 7486 0035

#237
The Dove Freehouse
Cuisines: Pub, Belgian
Average price: £11-25
Area: Broadway Market,
London Fields
Address: 24-26 Broadway Market
London E8 4QJ
Phone: +44 20 7275 7617

#238
Le Beaujolais
Cuisines: Wine Bar, French
Average price: £26-45
Area: Covent Garden
Address: 25 Litchfield Street
London WC2H 9NJ
Phone: +44 20 7836 2955

#239
Clutch
Cuisines: Breakfast & Brunch,
Chicken Wings
Average price: £11-25
Area: Shoreditch, Bethnal Green
Address: 4 Ravenscroft Street
London E2 7QG
Phone: +44 20 7098 0808

#240
Arancina
Cuisines: Italian, Pizza
Average price: Under £10
Area: Notting Hill
Address: 19 Pembridge Road
London W11 3HG
Phone: +44 20 7221 7776

#241
Siam Central
Cuisines: Thai
Average price: £11-25
Area: Fitzrovia
Address: 14 Charlotte Street
London W1T 2LX
Phone: +44 20 7436 7460

#242
The Dovetail
Cuisines: Pub, Belgian
Average price: £11-25
Area: Clerkenwell
Address: 9-10 Jerusalem Passage
London EC1V 4JP
Phone: +44 20 7490 7321

#243
Hummus Bros
Cuisines: Middle Eastern,
Greek, Mediterranean
Average price: Under £10
Area: Soho
Address: 88 Wardour Street
London W1F 0TH
Phone: +44 20 7734 1311

#244
Carpenter's Arms
Cuisines: Gastropub
Average price: £11-25
Area: Shoreditch, Bethnal Green
Address: 73 Cheshire Street
London E2 6EG
Phone: +44 20 7739 6342

#245
Phoenix Cinema
Cuisines: Cinema, Cafe
Average price: £11-25
Area: East Finchley, Fortis Green, Muswell
Hill
Address: 52 High Rd
London N2 9PJ
Phone: +44 20 8444 6789

#246
Babur
Cuisines: Indian, Fast Food
Average price: £26-45
Area: Forest Hill
Address: 119 Brockley Rise
London SE23 1JP
Phone: +44 20 8291 2400

#247
Woodlands
Cuisines: Indian, Vegetarian, Vegan
Average price: £11-25
Area: Marylebone
Address: 77 Marylebone Lane
London W1U 2PS
Phone: +44 20 7486 3862

#248
Bibendum Restaurant
Cuisines: Seafood Market,
Coffee & Tea, European
Average price: Above £46
Area: Chelsea
Address: 81 Fulham Road
London SW3 6RD
Phone: +44 20 7581 5817

#249
Yoobi
Cuisines: Sushi Bar
Average price: Under £10
Area: Soho
Address: 38 Lexington Street
London W1F 0LL
Phone: +44 20 7287 9442

#250
Yming
Cuisines: Chinese
Average price: £26-45
Area: Bloomsbury
Address: 35-36 Greek Street
London W1D 5DL
Phone: +44 20 7734 2721

#251
Marcus Wareing at The Berkeley
Cuisines: French, European
Average price: Above £46
Area: Belgravia
Address: Wilton Place
London SW1X 7RL
Phone: +44 20 7235 1200

#252
Isarn
Cuisines: Thai, Bar
Average price: £11-25
Area: Angel, Islington
Address: 119 Upper Street
London N1 1QP
Phone: +44 20 7424 5153

#253
Trishna
Cuisines: Indian
Average price: £26-45
Area: Marylebone
Address: 15-17 Blandford Street
London W1U 3DG
Phone: +44 20 7935 5624

#254
Cafe Japan
Cuisines: Japanese, Sushi Bar
Average price: £11-25
Area: Golders Green
Address: 626 Finchley Road
London NW11 7RR
Phone: +44 20 8455 6854

#255
Powder Keg Diplomacy
Cuisines: Bar, British
Average price: £11-25
Area: Clapham Junction,
Wandsworth Common
Address: 147 St John's Hill
London SW11 1TQ
Phone: +44 20 7450 6457

#256
Pham Sushi
Cuisines: Fast Food, Japanese
Average price: £26-45
Area: Barbican
Address: 159 Whitecross Street
London EC1Y 8JL
Phone: +44 20 7251 6336

#257
Assenheims 56
Cuisines: Cafe, Sandwiches,
Latin American
Average price: £11-25
Area: The City
Address: 24 Copthall Avenue
London EC2R 7DN
Phone: +44 20 7628 3787

#258
Gökyüzü
Cuisines: Turkish
Average price: Under £10
Area: Harringay
Address: 26-27 Grand Parade
London N4 1LG
Phone: +44 20 8211 8406

#259
Mother Mash
Cuisines: British
Average price: Under £10
Area: Soho
Address: 26 Ganton Street
London W1F 7QZ
Phone: +44 20 7494 9644

#260
Maison d'être
Cuisines: Coffee & Tea,
Breakfast & Brunch
Average price: Under £10
Area: Islington
Address: 154 Canonbury Road
London N1 2UP
Phone: +44 20 7226 4711

#261
Kikuchi
Cuisines: Japanese
Average price: £26-45
Area: Fitzrovia
Address: 14 Hanway Street
London W1T 1UD
Phone: +44 20 7637 7720

#262
Momo
Cuisines: Moroccan, Bar,
Breakfast & Brunch
Average price: £26-45
Area: Piccadilly
Address: 25-27 Heddon Street
London W1B 4BH
Phone: +44 20 7434 4040

#263
Nobu London
Cuisines: Japanese, Sushi Bar
Average price: Above £46
Area: Mayfair
Address: 19 Old Park Lane
London W1K 1LB
Phone: +44 20 7447 4747

#264
Andrew Edmunds
Cuisines: European
Average price: £26-45
Area: Soho
Address: 46 Lexington Street
London W1F 0LP
Phone: +44 20 7437 5708

#265
Wild Honey
Cuisines: European
Average price: £26-45
Area: Marylebone, Mayfair, Piccadilly
Address: 12 St George Street
London W1S 2FB
Phone: +44 20 7758 9160

#266
Dinings
Cuisines: Sushi Bar, Japanese
Average price: Above £46
Area: Marylebone
Address: 22 Harcourt Street
London W1H 4HH
Phone: +44 20 7723 0666

#267
Zafferano
Cuisines: Italian
Average price: Above £46
Area: Belgravia
Address: 15 Lowndes Street
London SW1X 9EY
Phone: +44 20 7235 5800

#268
Original Lahore Kebab House
Cuisines: Indian, Pakistani, Halal
Average price: £11-25
Area: Whitechapel
Address: 2-10 Umberston Street
London E1 1PY
Phone: +44 20 7481 9738

#269
Chilango Cuisines:
Mexican **Average price:**
Under £10
Area: Angel, Islington
Address: 27 Upper Street
London N1 0PN
Phone: +44 20 7704 2123

#270
Ekin Barbeque House
Cuisines: Barbeque, Turkish
Average price: Under £10
Area: Kilburn
Address: 240 Belsize Road
London NW6 4BT
Phone: +44 20 7624 7570

#271
Tapas Brindisa
Cuisines: Spanish, Basque
Average price: £11-25
Area: London Bridge
Address: 18-20 Southwark Street
London SE1 1TJ
Phone: +44 20 7407 1036

#272
Nando's
Cuisines: Portuguese, Chicken Wings
Average price: £11-25
Area: Marylebone
Address: 113 Baker Street
London W1U 6RS
Phone: +44 20 3075 1044

#273
The Ship
Cuisines: British, Pub
Average price: £11-25
Area: Wandsworth
Address: 41 Jews Row
London SW18 1TB
Phone: +44 20 8870 9667

#274
Byron
Cuisines: American, Burgers
Average price: £11-25
Area: South Kensington
Address: 75 Gloucester Road
London SW7 4SS
Phone: +44 20 7244 0700

#275
Byron
Cuisines: American, Burgers
Average price: £11-25
Area: Soho
Address: 97-99 Wardour Street
London W1F 0UD
Phone: +44 20 7434 2505

#276
Govinda's Restaurant
Cuisines: Vegetarian, Himalayan/Nepalese
Average price: Under £10
Area: Soho
Address: 10 Soho Street
London W1D 3DL
Phone: +44 20 7440 5229

#277
Tokyo Diner
Cuisines: Japanese
Average price: £11-25
Area: Chinatown
Address: 2 Newport Place
London WC2H 7JP

#278
Boisdale of Belgravia
Cuisines: British, Lounge, Jazz & Blues
Average price: £26-45
Area: Belgravia
Address: 15 Eccleston Street
London SW1W 9LX
Phone: +44 20 7730 6922

#279
Daquise
Cuisines: Polish, European
Average price: £26-45
Area: South Kensington
Address: 20 Thurloe Street
London SW7 2LT
Phone: +44 20 7589 6117

#280
Al Arez
Cuisines: Middle Eastern, Hookah Bar
Average price: £11-25
Area: Paddington
Address: 101 Edgware Road
London W2 2HX
Phone: +44 20 7262 4833

#281
Daddy Donkey
Cuisines: Mexican, Food Stands
Average price: Under £10
Area: Farringdon
Address: 50b Leather Lane
London EC1N 7TP
Phone: +44 20 7404 4173

#282
Caravan Kings Cross
Cuisines: Breakfast & Brunch,
Coffee & Tea, British
Average price: £11-25
Area: King's Cross
Address: 1 Granary Square
London N1C 4AA
Phone: +44 20 7101 7661

#283
The Breakfast Club
Cuisines: Breakfast & Brunch, American,
Coffee & Tea
Average price: £11-25
Area: Hoxton, Hoxton Square
Address: 2-4 Rufus Street
London N1 6PE
Phone: +44 20 7729 5252

#284
Locanda Locatelli
Cuisines: Italian
Average price: Above £46
Area: Marylebone
Address: 8 Seymour Street
London W1H 7JZ
Phone: +44 20 7935 9088

#285
The Providores Restaurant
Cuisines: European, Wine Bar, Breakfast
& Brunch
Average price: £11-25
Area: Marylebone
Address: 109 Marylebone High Street
London W1U 4RX
Phone: +44 20 7935 6175

#286
My Village Café
Cuisines: Vegetarian, Vegan
Average price: Under £10
Area: Camden Town
Address: 37 Chalk Farm Road
London NW1 8AJ
Phone: +44 20 3489 2293

#287
Diwana
Cuisines: Indian, Vegetarian
Average price: Under £10
Area: Euston
Address: 121 Drummond Street
London NW1 2HL
Phone: +44 20 7387 5556

#288
Greenwich Market
Cuisines: Farmers Market, Food Stands
Average price: £11-25
Area: Greenwich
Address: 5B Greenwich Market
London SE10 9HY
Phone: +44 20 8269 5096

#289
All Star Lanes
Cuisines: Bowling, American, Karaoke
Average price: £11-25
Area: Brick Lane, Shoreditch
Address: 95 Brick Lane
London E1 6QL
Phone: +44 20 7426 9200

#290
Meat Mission
Cuisines: Burgers
Average price: £11-25
Area: Hoxton, Hoxton Square
Address: 14-15 Hoxton Market
London N1 6HG
Phone: +44 20 7739 8212

#291
Cecconi's
Cuisines: Italian, Wine Bar
Average price: £11-25
Area: Piccadilly
Address: 5-5A Burlington Gardens
London W1S 3EP
Phone: +44 20 7434 1500

#292
Jak's
Cuisines: Mediterranean, Greek
Average price: £11-25
Area: Chelsea
Address: 77 Walton Street
London SW3 2HT
Phone: +44 20 7584 3441

#293
El Parador
Cuisines: Spanish, Basque
Average price: £11-25
Area: Euston, Camden Town
Address: 245 Eversholt Street
London NW1 1BA
Phone: +44 20 7387 2789

#294
Byron
Cuisines: Burgers, American
Average price: £11-25
Area: Angel, Islington
Address: 341 Upper Street
London N1 0PB
Phone: +44 20 7704 7620

#295
Gallipoli Again
Cuisines: Turkish
Average price: £11-25
Area: Angel, Islington
Address: 120 Upper Street
London N1 1QP
Phone: +44 20 7359 1578

#296
Little Georgia
Cuisines: Cafe
Average price: £11-25
Area: Bethnal Green, Broadway Market
Address: 87 Goldsmiths Row
London E2 8QR
Phone: +44 20 7739 8154

#297
Cah-Chi
Cuisines: Korean
Average price: £11-25
Area: Summerstown
Address: 394 Garratt Lane
London SW18 4HP
Phone: +44 20 8946 8811

#298
Workshop Coffee Co.
Cuisines: Coffee & Tea, Cafe
Average price: Under £10
Area: Marylebone
Address: 75 Wigmore Street
London W1U 1QD

#299
Vinoteca
Cuisines: Wine Bar, European
Average price: £11-25
Area: Farringdon
Address: 7 St John Street
London EC1M 4AA
Phone: +44 20 7253 8786

#300
The Pavilion Cafe
Cuisines: Coffee & Tea,
Breakfast & Brunch
Average price: £11-25
Area: Victoria Park
Address: Victoria Park
London E9 7DE
Phone: +44 20 8980 0030

#301
Recipease
Cuisines: Cafe, Cooking School
Average price: £11-25
Area: Notting Hill
Address: 92-94 Notting Hill Gate
London W11 3QB
Phone: +44 20 3375 5398

#302
The Troubadour
Cuisines: British, Music Venues
Average price: £11-25
Area: Earls Court
Address: 263-7 Old Brompton Road
London SW5 9JA
Phone: +44 20 7370 1434

#303
Rock & Sole Plaice
Cuisines: Fish & Chips
Average price: £11-25
Area: Covent Garden
Address: 47 Endell Street
London WC2H 9AJ
Phone: +44 20 7836 3785

#304
The River Cafe
Cuisines: Italian
Average price: Above £46
Area: Fulham
Address: Rainville Road
London W6 9HA
Phone: +44 20 7386 4200

#305
Caffe Vergnano 1882
Cuisines: Coffee & Tea, Cafe
Average price: £11-25
Area: Covent Garden
Address: 62 Charing Cross Road
London WC2H 0BB
Phone: +44 20 7240 3512

#306
The Red Fort
Cuisines: Indian
Average price: £26-45
Area: Soho
Address: 77 Dean Street
London W1D 3SH
Phone: +44 20 7437 2525

#307
Sandwich Shop
Cuisines: Sandwiches
Average price: Under £10
Area: Kensington
Address: 54 Gloucester Road
London SW7 4QT
Phone: +44 20 7589 2849

#308
La Trompette
Cuisines: French
Average price: £26-45
Area: Chiswick
Address: 3-7 Devonshire Road
London W4 2EU
Phone: +44 20 8747 1836

#309
Roti Joupa
Cuisines: Fast Food, Caribbean
Average price: £11-25
Area: Clapham, Clapham Common
Address: 12 Clapham High Street
London SW4 7UT
Phone: +44 20 7627 8637

#310
The Modern Pantry
Cuisines: Deli, European,
Breakfast & Brunch
Average price: £11-25
Area: Clerkenwell
Address: 47-48 St John's Square
London EC1V 4JJ
Phone: +44 20 7553 9210

#311
Brawn
Cuisines: European
Average price: £26-45
Area: Shoreditch, Bethnal Green
Address: 49 Columbia Road
London E2 7RG
Phone: +44 20 7729 5692

#312
Gaucho
Cuisines: Argentine, Steakhouse
Average price: Above £46
Area: Piccadilly
Address: 25 Swallow Street
London W1B 4QR
Phone: +44 20 7734 4040

#313
Fino
Cuisines: Spanish, Basque, Tapas
Average price: £26-45
Area: Fitzrovia
Address: 33 Charlotte Street
London W1T 1RR
Phone: +44 20 7813 8010

#314
Chutneys
Cuisines: Indian, Vegetarian, Pakistani
Average price: Under £10
Area: Euston
Address: 124 Drummond Street
London NW1 2PA
Phone: +44 20 7388 0604

#315
Kati Roll Company
Cuisines: Indian
Average price: Under £10
Area: Soho
Address: 24 Poland Street
London W1F 8QL
Phone: +44 20 7287 4787

#316
Mangal Ocakbasi
Cuisines: Turkish
Average price: £11-25
Area: Dalston
Address: 10 Arcola Street
London E8 2DJ
Phone: +44 20 7275 8981

#317
The Bull & Last
Cuisines: Bar, Gastropub
Average price: £26-45
Area: Parliament Hill/Dartmouth Park
Address: 168 Highgate Road
London NW5 1QS
Phone: +44 20 7267 3641

#318
Moro Restaurant
Cuisines: Spanish, Basque
Average price: £26-45
Area: Clerkenwell
Address: 34-36 Exmouth Market
London EC1R 4QE
Phone: +44 20 7833 8336

#319
The Square
Cuisines: French, European
Average price: Above £46
Area: Mayfair
Address: 6-10 Bruton Street
London W1J 6PU
Phone: +44 20 7495 7100

#320
Kua 'Aina
Cuisines: Hawaiian, Burgers,
Breakfast & Brunch
Average price: £11-25
Area: Soho
Address: 26 Fouberts Place
London W1F 7PP
Phone: +44 20 7287 7474

#321
Makoto Sushi Bar
Cuisines: Japanese, Sushi Bar
Average price: £11-25
Area: Chiswick
Address: 4 Devonshire Road
London W4 2HD
Phone: +44 20 8987 3180

#322
La Porte Des Indes
Cuisines: Indian
Average price: £26-45
Area: Marylebone
Address: 32 Bryanston Street
London W1H 7EG
Phone: +44 20 7224 0055

#323
Patogh
Cuisines: Persian/Iranian
Average price: Under £10
Area: Marylebone
Address: 8 Crawford Place
London W1H 5NE
Phone: +44 20 7262 4015

#324
Lucky Voice Karaoke
Cuisines: Japanese, Karaoke, Pizza
Average price: £26-45
Area: Soho
Address: 52 Poland Street
London W1F 7NQ
Phone: +44 20 7439 3660

#325
Marine Ices
Cuisines: Ice Cream, Italian
Average price: £11-25
Area: Camden Town, Chalk Farm
Address: 8 Haverstock Hill
London NW3 2BL
Phone: +44 20 7267 2776

#326
Lemonia
Cuisines: Greek
Average price: £11-25
Area: Chalk Farm, Primrose Hill
Address: 89 Regents Park Road
London NW1 8UY
Phone: +44 20 7586 7454

#327
Meze Mangal
Cuisines: Turkish
Average price: £11-25
Area: Lewisham, St Johns
Address: 245 Lewisham Way
London SE4 1XF
Phone: +44 20 8694 8099

#328
Lisboa Patisserie
Cuisines: Portuguese, Bakery, Cafe
Average price: Under £10
Area: Kensal Town
Address: 57 Golborne Road
London W10 5NR
Phone: +44 20 8968 5242

#329
222 Veggie Vegan
Cuisines: Vegetarian, Vegan
Average price: £11-25
Area: Barons Court, West Kensington
Address: 222 N End Road
London W14 9NU
Phone: +44 20 7381 2322

#330
Wahaca
Cuisines: Mexican
Average price: £11-25
Area: Shepherd's Bush, White City
Address: 1074 Westfield Shopping Centre,
London W12 7GD
Phone: +44 20 8749 4517

#331
The Garrison
Cuisines: Pub, British
Average price: £26-45
Area: Borough
Address: 99 Bermondsey Street
London SE1 3XB
Phone: +44 20 7089 9355

#332
The Porterhouse
Cuisines: Pub, Irish
Average price: £11-25
Area: Covent Garden, Strand
Address: 21-22 Maiden Lane
London WC2E 7NA
Phone: +44 20 7379 7917

#333
Cafe 338
Cuisines: Cafe
Average price: Under £10
Area: Shoreditch, Bethnal Green
Address: 338 Bethnal Green Road
London E2 0AG
Phone: +44 4402 077398

#334
Zerodegrees Restaurant
Cuisines: Bar, Italian, Pizza
Average price: £11-25
Area: Blackheath
Address: 29 Montpelier Vale
London SE3 0TJ
Phone: +44 20 8852 5619

#335
Jack's at the Junction
Cuisines: Breakfast & Brunch, Diner
Average price: Under £10
Area: Battersea, Clapham,
Clapham Junction
Address: 252 Lavender Hill
London SW11 1LJ
Phone: +44 20 7228 9111

#336
Shoryu Ramen
Cuisines: Japanese, Ethnic Food, Gluten-
Free
Average price: £11-25
Area: St James's
Address: 9 Regent Street
London SW1Y 4LR

#337
Jakobs
Cuisines: Bakery, Mediterranean, Greek
Average price: £11-25
Area: Kensington
Address: 20 Gloucester Road
London SW7 4RB
Phone: +44 20 7581 9292

#338
Zaffrani Indian Dining
Cuisines: Indian, Pakistani
Average price: £26-45
Area: Islington
Address: 47 Cross Street
London N1 2BB
Phone: +44 20 7226 5522

#339
Ecco Cafe
Cuisines: Cafe
Average price: Under £10
Area: Covent Garden
Address: 186 Drury Lane
London WC2B 5QD
Phone: +44 20 7404 3555

#340
Jin Kichi
Cuisines: Japanese, Sushi Bar
Average price: £11-25
Area: Hampstead Village
Address: 73 Heath Street
London NW3 6UG
Phone: +44 20 7794 6158

#341
Sushi Say Cuisines:
Japanese **Average
price:** £11-25
Area: Brondesbury, Cricklewood
Address: 33b Walm Lane
London NW2 5SH
Phone: +44 20 8459 2971

#342
Chipotle
Cuisines: Mexican
Average price: Under £10
Area: Covent Garden, Strand
Address: 92-93 St Martins Lane
London WC2N 4AP
Phone: +44 20 7836 7838

#343
Gurkhas
Cuisines: Himalayan/Nepalese
Average price: £11-25
Area: Tooting, Tooting Bec
Address: 1 The Boulevard
London SW17 7BW
Phone: +44 20 8675 1188

#344
Goring Hotel
Cuisines: Hotel, British
Average price: Above £46
Area: Victoria
Address: 15 Beeston Place
London SW1W 0JW
Phone: +44 20 7396 9000

#345
Eat Tokyo
Cuisines: Japanese, Sushi Bar, Buffet
Average price: £11-25
Area: Notting Hill
Address: 18 Hillgate Street
London W8 7SR
Phone: +44 20 7792 9313

#346
Benares Restaurant & Bar
Cuisines: Indian
Average price: Above £46
Area: Mayfair
Address: 12a Berkeley Square
London W1J 6BS
Phone: +44 20 7629 8886

#347
The Breakfast Club
Cuisines: Coffee & Tea,
Breakfast & Brunch, American
Average price: £11-25
Area: Soho
Address: 33 D'Arblay Street
London W1F 8EU
Phone: +44 20 7434 2571

#348
Mestizo
Cuisines: Mexican, Bar
Average price: £11-25
Area: Euston
Address: 103 Hampstead Road
London NW1 3EL
Phone: +44 20 7387 4064

#349
Duke Of Cambridge
Cuisines: Pub, Gastropub,
Organic Store
Average price: £26-45
Area: Angel, Islington
Address: 30 St Peters Street
London N1 8JT
Phone: +44 20 7359 3066

#350
Made in Italy
Cuisines: Italian
Average price: £11-25
Area: Chelsea
Address: 249 King's Road
London SW3 5EL
Phone: +44 20 7352 1880

#351
Randall & Aubin
Cuisines: Seafood, British
Average price: £26-45
Area: Soho
Address: 16 Brewer Street
London W1F 0SQ
Phone: +44 20 7287 4447

#352
Cinnamon Kitchen & Anise
Cuisines: Indian
Average price: £26-45
Area: Aldgate
Address: 9 Devonshire Square
London EC2M 4YL
Phone: +44 20 7626 5000

#353
The Seashell of Lisson Grove
Cuisines: Seafood, Fish & Chips
Average price: £11-25
Area: Lisson Grove
Address: 49-51 Lisson Grove
London NW1 6UH
Phone: +44 20 7224 9000

#354
Barhu
Cuisines: Szechuan
Average price: £26-45
Area: Bloomsbury
Address: 28 Frith Street
London W1D 5LF
Phone: +44 20 7287 8858

#355
Tsuru
Cuisines: Japanese, Sushi Bar
Average price: £11-25
Area: Southwark
Address: 4 Canvey Street
London SE1 9AN
Phone: +44 20 7928 2228

#356
The Eagle
Cuisines: Gastropub, Pub, British
Average price: £11-25
Area: Bloomsbury
Address: 159 Farringdon Road
London EC1R 3AL
Phone: +44 20 7837 1353

#357
Lola & Simon
Cuisines: Argentine, Mediterranean
Average price: £26-45
Area: Hammersmith, Ravenscourt Park
Address: 278 King Street
London W6 0SP
Phone: +44 20 8563 0300

#358
Little Bay West Hampstead
Cuisines: French, Mediterranean
Average price: £11-25
Area: Kilburn
Address: 228 Belsize Road
London NW6 4BT
Phone: +44 20 7372 4699

#359
Santa Maria del Sur
Cuisines: Steakhouse, Argentine,
Latin American
Average price: £26-45
Area: Battersea, Clapham
Address: 129 Queenstown Road
London SW8 3RH
Phone: +44 20 7622 2088

#360
The Bridge
Cuisines: Coffee & Tea,
Sandwiches, Lounge
Average price: £11-25
Area: Hoxton
Address: 15 Kingsland Road
London E2 8AA
Phone: +44 871 963 4200

#361
The Cow
Cuisines: British, Gastropub
Average price: £26-45
Area: Bayswater
Address: 89 Westbourne Park Road
London W2 5QH
Phone: +44 20 7221 0021

#362
Navarro's Restaurant
Cuisines: Spanish
Average price: £11-25
Area: Fitzrovia
Address: 67 Charlotte Street
London W1T 4PH
Phone: +44 20 7637 7713

#363
Marquis Of Westminster
Cuisines: British, Pub, Cocktail Bar
Average price: £11-25
Area: Pimlico
Address: 50 Warwick Way
London SW1V 1RY
Phone: +44 20 7828 1700

#364
The Lock Tavern
Cuisines: Pub, British
Average price: £11-25
Area: Camden Town
Address: 35 Chalk Farm Road
London NW1 8AJ
Phone: +44 20 7482 7163

#365
Café 1001
Cuisines: Coffee & Tea,
Music Venues, Burgers
Average price: £11-25
Area: Brick Lane, Shoreditch
Address: 91 Brick Lane
London E1 6QL
Phone: +44 20 7247 9679

#366
Woody Grill
Cuisines: Fast Food,
Mediterranean, Turkish
Average price: Under £10
Area: Camden Town
Address: 1A Camden Road
London NW1 9LG
Phone: +44 20 8616 9587

#367
Seoul Bakery
Cuisines: Korean
Average price: Under £10
Area: Bloomsbury
Address: 55 St Giles High Street
London WC2H 8LH
Phone: +44 20 7240 0877

#368
Pierre Victoire
Cuisines: French
Average price: £11-25
Area: Soho
Address: 5 Dean Street
London W1D 3RQ
Phone: +44 20 7287 4582

#369
Meat Liquor
Cuisines: Burgers
Average price: £11-25
Area: Marylebone
Address: 74 Welbeck Street
London W1G 0BA
Phone: +44 20 7224 4239

#370
Pizza Pilgrims
Cuisines: Pizza
Average price: £11-25
Area: Soho
Address: 11 Dean Street
London W1D 3RP
Phone: +44 20 7287 8964

#371
Masala Zone
Cuisines: Indian, Vegetarian, Halal
Average price: £11-25
Area: Soho
Address: 9 Marshall Street
London W1F 7ER
Phone: +44 20 7287 9966

#372
Benito's Hat
Cuisines: Mexican
Average price: Under £10
Area: Fitzrovia
Address: 56 Goodge Street
London W1T 4NB
Phone: +44 20 7637 3732

#373
Hibiscus Restaurant
Cuisines: French
Average price: Above £46
Area: Marylebone, Piccadilly
Address: 29 Maddox Street
London W1S 2PA
Phone: +44 20 7629 2999

#374
Wright Brothers
Cuisines: Seafood
Average price: £26-45
Area: London Bridge
Address: 11 Stoney Street
London SE1 9AD
Phone: +44 20 7403 9554

#375
Portal
Cuisines: Portuguese,
Mediterranean, Wine Bar
Average price: £26-45
Area: Farringdon
Address: 88 St John Street
London EC1M 4EH
Phone: +44 20 7253 6950

#376
Laughing Gravy
Cuisines: Pub, British
Average price: £26-45
Area: Southwark
Address: 154 Blackfriars Road
London SE1 8EN
Phone: +44 20 7998 1707

#377
Make Mine
Cuisines: Cafe
Average price: £11-25
Area: Marylebone
Address: 314 Regent Street
London W1B 3BB
Phone: +44 20 7636 1308

#378
Dabbous
Cuisines: European, Bar
Average price: Above £46
Area: Fitzrovia
Address: 39 Whitfield Street
London W1T 2SF
Phone: +44 20 7323 1544

#379
Daylesford Organic
Cuisines: Specialty Food, British
Average price: £26-45
Area: Belgravia
Address: 44b Pimlico Road
London SW1W 8LP
Phone: +44 20 7881 8060

#380
Beatroot Cafe
Cuisines: Coffee & Tea, Vegan
Average price: Under £10
Area: Soho
Address: 92 Berwick Street
London W1F 0QD
Phone: +44 20 7437 8591

#381
Wasabi
Cuisines: Fast Food, Japanese,
Sushi Bar
Average price: Under £10
Area: Marylebone
Address: 439 Oxford Street
London W1C 2PN
Phone: +44 20 7493 6422

#382
J+A Café
Cuisines: Coffee & Tea,
Breakfast & Brunch
Average price: £11-25
Area: Clerkenwell
Address: 4 Sutton Lane
London EC1M 5PU
Phone: +44 20 7490 2992

#383
Yoshino
Cuisines: Japanese
Average price: £26-45
Area: Piccadilly
Address: 3 Piccadilly Place
London W1J 0DB
Phone: +44 20 7287 6622

#384
Blue Elephant
Cuisines: Thai
Average price: £26-45
Area: Fulham
Address: The Boulevard
London SW6 2UB
Phone: +44 20 7751 3111

#385
Papaya
Cuisines: Thai
Average price: Under £10
Area: Soho
Address: 14 St Anne's Court
London W1F 0BD
Phone: +44 20 7734 8994

#386
Balthazar
Cuisines: American, French
Average price: £11-25
Area: Covent Garden, Strand
Address: 4-6 Russell Street
London WC2B 5HZ
Phone: +44 20 3301 1155

#387
Criterion Restaurant
Cuisines: European
Average price: £26-45
Area: Piccadilly
Address: 224 Piccadilly
London W1J 9HP
Phone: +44 20 7930 0488

#388
Vapiano
Cuisines: Italian, Pizza
Average price: £11-25
Area: Southwark
Address: 90 B Southwark street
London SE1 0FD
Phone: +44 20 7593 2010

#389
Bosphorus Kebabs
Cuisines: Middle Eastern, Fast Food
Average price: Under £10
Area: South Kensington
Address: 59 Old Brompton Road
London SW7 3JS
Phone: +44 20 7584 4048

#390
Sacred
Cuisines: Coffee & Tea, Sandwiches
Average price: £11-25
Area: Soho
Address: 13 Ganton Street
London W1F 9BL
Phone: +44 20 7734 1415

#391
Candid Café
Cuisines: Coffee & Tea, Greek,
Mediterranean
Average price: £11-25
Area: Angel, Islington
Address: 3 Torrens Street
London EC1V 1NQ
Phone: +44 20 7837 4237

#392
Annie's
Cuisines: European
Average price: £11-25
Area: Chiswick, Kew
Address: 162 Thames Road
London W4 3QS
Phone: +44 20 8994 9080

#393
Arancina
Cuisines: Pizza, Italian, Fast Food
Average price: £11-25
Area: Bayswater
Address: 19 Westbourne Grove
London W2 4UA
Phone: +44 20 7792 9777

#394
Hereford Road
Cuisines: British
Average price: £26-45
Area: Notting Hill
Address: 3 Hereford Road
London W2 4AB
Phone: +44 20 7727 1144

#395
Levant
Cuisines: Vegetarian, Fast Food
Average price: Above £46
Area: Marylebone
Address: 76 Wigmore Street
London W1U 2SJ
Phone: +44 20 7224 1111

#396
Negril
Cuisines: Caribbean, Juice Bar
Average price: £11-25
Area: Brixton, Brixton Hill
Address: 132 Brixton Hill
London SW2 1RS
Phone: +44 20 8674 8798

#397
The Cookbook Cafe
Cuisines: Breakfast & Brunch, British
Average price: £26-45
Area: Mayfair
Address: 1 Hamilton Place Park Lane
London W1J 7QY
Phone: +44 20 7318 8563

#398
Abu Zaad
Cuisines: Middle Eastern
Average price: £11-25
Area: Shepherd's Bush
Address: 29 Uxbridge Road
London W12 8LH
Phone: +44 20 8749 5107

#399
Market
Cuisines: British, Bistro
Average price: £26-45
Area: Camden Town
Address: 43 Parkway
London NW1 7PN
Phone: +44 20 7267 9700

#400
Alforno Restaurant
Cuisines: Italian
Average price: £11-25
Area: Wimbledon
Address: 2a Kings Road
London SW19 8QN
Phone: +44 20 8540 5710

#401
The Anchor and Hope
Cuisines: British
Average price: £11-25
Area: Southwark, Waterloo
Address: 36 The Cut
London SE1 8LP
Phone: +44 20 7928 9898

#402
Cafe Mama Pho
Cuisines: Vietnamese
Average price: Under £10
Area: Deptford
Address: 24 Evelyn Street
London SE8 5DG
Phone: +44 20 8305 6649

#403
St. Moritz Restaurant
Cuisines: Fondue
Average price: £26-45
Area: Soho
Address: 161 Wardour St
London W1F 8WJ
Phone: +44 20 7734 3324

#404
Coya
Cuisines: Peruvian
Average price: Above £46
Area: Mayfair
Address: 118 Piccadilly
London W1J 7NW
Phone: +44 20 7042 7118

#405
Angels & Gypsies
Cuisines: Spanish
Average price: £11-25
Area: Camberwell
Address: 29-33 Camberwell Church
Street, London SE5 8TR
Phone: +44 20 7703 5984

#406
Nusa
Cuisines: Soup, Fast Food
Average price: Under £10
Area: Barbican
Address: 9 Old Street
London EC1V 9HL
Phone: +44 20 7253 3135

#407
Adobo
Cuisines: Mexican, Fast Food
Average price: Under £10
Area: Bloomsbury
Address: 87 High Holborn
London WC1V 6LS
Phone: +44 20 7404 6976

#408
The Toucan
Cuisines: Pub, Irish
Average price: £11-25
Area: Soho
Address: 19 Carlisle Street
London W1D 3BY
Phone: +44 20 7437 4123

#409
Gaucho
Cuisines: Argentine, Steakhouse
Average price: Above £46
Area: London Bridge
Address: 2 More London Riverside
London SE1 2AP
Phone: +44 20 7407 5222

#410
Chicken Shop
Cuisines: Cafe
Average price: £11-25
Area: Kentish Town, Parliament
Hill/Dartmouth Park
Address: 79 Highgate Road
London NW5 1TL
Phone: +44 20 3310 2020

#411
Gourmet Burger Kitchen
Cuisines: Fast Food, American
Average price: £11-25
Area: Bayswater
Address: 50 Westbourne Grove
London W2 5SH
Phone: +44 20 7243 4344

#412
Mews Of Mayfair
Cuisines: British, Steakhouse, Brasserie
Average price: £26-45
Area: Marylebone
Address: 10 Lancashire Court
London W1S 1EY
Phone: +44 20 7518 9388

#413
Cây Tre
Cuisines: Vietnamese
Average price: £11-25
Area: Hoxton, Hoxton Square
Address: 301 Old Street
London EC1V 9LA
Phone: +44 20 7729 8662

#414
The Elk in the Woods
Cuisines: Pub, Sandwiches, British
Average price: £11-25
Area: Angel, Islington
Address: 39 Camden Passage
London N1 8EA
Phone: +44 20 7226 3535

#415
Montgomery Place
Cuisines: Bar, Tapas Bar
Average price: £11-25
Area: Notting Hill
Address: 31 Kensington Park Road
London W11 2EU
Phone: +44 20 7792 3921

#416
Delhi Grill
Cuisines: Indian
Average price: £11-25
Area: Islington
Address: 21 Chapel Market
London N1 9EZ
Phone: +44 20 7278 8100

#417
Itsu
Cuisines: Sushi Bar
Average price: £11-25
Area: Piccadilly
Address: 167 Piccadilly
London W1J 9EG
Phone: +44 20 7495 4048

#418
Cafe Spice Namaste
Cuisines: Indian
Average price: £26-45
Area: Whitechapel
Address: 16 Prescot Street
London E1 8AZ
Phone: +44 20 7488 9242

#419
Vapiano Cuisines:
Italian **Average price:**
£11-25
Area: Fitzrovia
Address: 19-21 Great Portland Street
London W1W 8QB
Phone: +44 20 7268 0082

#420
Taza Sandwich
Cuisines: Fast Food
Average price: Under £10
Area: Bayswater
Address: 35a Queensway
London W2 4QJ
Phone: +44 20 7727 7420

#421
Sophie's Steakhouse & Bar
Cuisines: Steakhouse, Burgers
Average price: £26-45
Area: Covent Garden, Strand
Address: 29-31 Wellington Street
London WC2E 7DB
Phone: +44 20 7836 8836

#422
**Fortnum and Mason
Diamond Jubilee Tea Salon**
Cuisines: Desserts, British, Tea Room
Average price: £26-45
Area: Piccadilly
Address: 181 Piccadilly
London W1A 1ER
Phone: +44 845 300 1707

#423
Pimlico Fresh
Cuisines: Coffee & Tea,
Breakfast & Brunch
Average price: Under £10
Area: Victoria
Address: 85 Wilton Road
London SW1V 1DE
Phone: +44 20 7932 0030

#424
Foxcroft and Ginger
Cuisines: Coffee & Tea, Bakery, Pizza
Average price: £11-25
Area: Soho
Address: 3 Berwick Street
London W1F 0DR
Phone: +44 20 3602 3371

#425
Rainforest Creations
Cuisines: Cafe
Average price: Under £10
Area: Spitalfields
Address: Brushfield Street
London E1 6BG
Phone: +44 7985 235219

#426
Ohayo Sushi
Cuisines: Sushi Bar
Average price: £11-25
Area: Wandsworth
Address: 3 Keswick Broadway
London SW15 2RB
Phone: +44 7517 577799

#427
Village East
Cuisines: Wine Bar, European, British
Average price: £26-45
Area: Borough
Address: 171-173 Bermondsey Street
London SE1 3UW
Phone: +44 20 7357 6082

#428
La Famiglia
Cuisines: Italian, Gluten-Free
Average price: £26-45
Area: Chelsea
Address: 7 Langton Street
London SW10 0JL
Phone: +44 20 7352 6095

#429
Akari
Cuisines: Japanese, Bar
Average price: £11-25
Area: Canonbury
Address: 196 Essex Road
London N1 8LZ
Phone: +44 20 7226 9943

#430
The Drunken Monkey
Cuisines: Dim Sum, Lounge,
Cocktail Bar
Average price: £11-25
Area: Liverpool Street / Broadgate
Address: 222 Shoreditch High Street
London E1 6PJ
Phone: +44 20 7392 9606

#431
Hedone
Cuisines: British
Average price: Above £46
Area: Chiswick
Address: 301-303 Chiswick High Road
London W4 4HH
Phone: +44 20 8747 0377

#432
Fez Mangal
Cuisines: Turkish
Average price: £11-25
Area: Notting Hill
Address: 104 Ladbroke Grove
London W11 1PY
Phone: +44 20 7229 3010

#433
Honey & Co.
Cuisines: Middle Eastern
Average price: £11-25
Area: Fitzrovia
Address: 25a Warren Street
London W1T 5LZ
Phone: +44 20 7388 6175

#434
Gig's
Cuisines: Fish & Chips, Greek,
Fast Food
Average price: £11-25
Area: Fitzrovia
Address: 12 Tottenham Street
London W1T 4RE
Phone: +44 20 7636 1424

#435
Four Seasons
Cuisines: Chinese
Average price: £11-25
Area: Bayswater
Address: 84 Queensway
London W2 3RL
Phone: +44 20 7229 4320

#436
Grosvenor House
JW Marriott Hotel
Cuisines: Hotel, Cafe
Average price: £26-45
Area: Mayfair
Address: 86-90 Park Lane
London W1K 7TN
Phone: +44 20 7499 6363

#437
Ace Café London
Cuisines: Diner, Music Venues
Average price: Under £10
Area: Hangar Lane
Address: N Circular Road
London NW10 7UD
Phone: +44 20 8961 1000

#438
The London Particular
Cuisines: Cafe, British
Average price: £11-25
Area: New Cross
Address: 399 New Cross Road
London SE14 6LA
Phone: +44 20 8692 6149

#439
Kennedy's Of Goswell Road
Cuisines: Fish & Chips, Fast Food
Average price: £11-25
Area: Barbican
Address: 184-186 Goswell Road
London EC1V 7DT
Phone: +44 20 7251 0057

#440
Royal China
Cuisines: Dim Sum
Average price: £11-25
Area: Bayswater
Address: 13 Queensway
London W2 4QJ
Phone: +44 20 7221 2535

#441
The Gun
Cuisines: British, Mediterranean, Pub
Average price: £11-25
Area: Isle of Dogs, West India Docks
Address: 27 Coldharbour
London E14 9NS
Phone: +44 20 7515 5222

#442
The Abingdon
Cuisines: Gastropub, American
Average price: £26-45
Area: Kensington
Address: 54 Abingdon Road
London W8 6AP
Phone: +44 20 7937 3339

#443
Tramshed
Cuisines: British, Steakhouse
Average price: £11-25
Area: Hoxton
Address: 32 Rivington Street
London EC2A 3LX
Phone: +44 20 7749 0478

#444
Camera Cafe
Cuisines: Cafe
Average price: Under £10
Area: Bloomsbury
Address: 44 Museum Street
London WC1A 1LY
Phone: +44 7887 930826

#445
Naru
Cuisines: Korean
Average price: £11-25
Area: Covent Garden
Address: 230 Shaftsbury Avenue
London WC2H 8EG
Phone: +44 20 7379 7962

#446
Rabot Estate
Cuisines: Chocolatiers & Shop, Cafe
Average price: £11-25
Area: London Bridge
Address: 2 Stoney Street
London SE1 9AA
Phone: +44 20 7403 9852

#447
Coach & Horses
Cuisines: Pub, Vegan, Vegetarian
Average price: £11-25
Area: Bloomsbury
Address: 29 Greek Street
London W1D 5DH
Phone: +44 20 7437 5920

#448
The Bull Steak Expert
Cuisines: Argentine, Steakhouse
Average price: £26-45
Area: Bloomsbury
Address: 54 Red Lion Street
London WC1R 4PD
Phone: +44 20 7242 0708

#449
La Gaffe
Cuisines: Hotel, Italian
Average price: £11-25
Area: Hampstead Village
Address: 107-111 Heath Street
London NW3 6SS
Phone: +44 20 7435 8965

#450
R Garcia & Sons
Foods and Wines of Spain
Cuisines: Deli, Spanish, Beer,
Wine, Spirits
Average price: £26-45
Area: Notting Hill
Address: 248-250 Portobello Road
London W11 1LL
Phone: +44 20 7221 6119

#451
White Rabbit
Cuisines: British
Average price: £26-45
Area: De Beauvoir, Kingsland
Address: 15-16 Bradbury Street
London N16 8JN
Phone: +44 20 7682 0163

#452
Yum Cha Silks & Spice
Cuisines: Dim Sum, Karaoke
Average price: £11-25
Area: Camden Town
Address: 28 Chalk Farm Road
London NW1 8AG
Phone: +44 20 7482 2228

#453
The Grazing Goat
Cuisines: Gastropub, British
Average price: £11-25
Area: Marylebone
Address: 6 New Quebec Street
London W1H 7RQ
Phone: +44 20 7724 7243

#454
Kitchen W8
Cuisines: French
Average price: £26-45
Area: Kensington
Address: 11-13 Abingdon Road
London W8 6AH
Phone: +44 20 7937 0120

#455
The Jolly Butchers
Cuisines: Pub, Gastropub
Average price: £11-25
Area: Stoke Newington Central
Address: 204 Stoke Newington High
Street, London N16 7HU
Phone: +44 20 7249 9471

#456
Bruno's Deli
Cuisines: Italian, Delicatessen
Average price: Under £10
Area: St John's Wood
Address: 59A Abbey Road
London NW8 0AD
Phone: +44 20 7328 8692

#457
Sfizio Italian Bar and Caffe
Cuisines: Italian, Cafe, Pizza
Average price: £11-25
Area: Bloomsbury
Address: 35-37 Theobald's Road
London WC1X 8SP
Phone: +44 20 7831 1888

#458
E. Mono
Cuisines: Turkish, Fast Food
Average price: Under £10
Area: Kentish Town
Address: 287 Kentish Town Road
London NW5 2JS

#459
Rose Vegetarian Restaurant
Cuisines: Indian, Vegetarian
Average price: £11-25
Area: Kingsbury
Address: 532/534 Kingsbury Road
London NW9 9HH
Phone: +44 20 8905 0025

#460
Luigi's Delicatessen
Cuisines: Italian, Delicatessen
Average price: £11-25
Area: Southfields
Address: 349 Fulham Road
London SW10 9TW
Phone: +44 20 7735 27739

#461
Wok To Walk
Cuisines: Asian Fusion
Average price: Under £10
Area: Soho
Address: 4 Brewer Street
London W1F 0SB
Phone: +44 20 7287 8464

#462
Belgo Noord
Cuisines: Belgian
Average price: £11-25
Area: Camden Town, Chalk Farm
Address: 72 Chalk Farm Road
London NW1 8AN
Phone: +44 20 7267 0718

#463
Halepi
Cuisines: Greek, European
Average price: £11-25
Area: Bayswater
Address: 18 Leinster Terrace
London W2 3ET
Phone: +44 20 7262 1070

#464
Byron
Cuisines: Burgers
Average price: £11-25
Area: Hoxton, Hoxton Square
Address: 46 Hoxton Square
London N1 6BP
Phone: +44 20 7729 1416

#465
Tortilla
Cuisines: Mexican, Fast Food
Average price: £11-25
Area: Aldgate
Address: 28 Leadenhall Market
London EC3V 1LR
Phone: +44 20 7929 7837

#466
Fifteen
Cuisines: Mediterranean, Italian
Average price: Above £46
Area: Islington
Address: 15 Westland Place
London N1 7LP
Phone: +44 20 3375 1515

#467
E&O
Cuisines: Asian Fusion
Average price: £26-45
Area: Notting Hill
Address: 14 Blenheim Crescent
London W11 1NN
Phone: +44 20 7229 5454

#468
Marathon Kebabs
Cuisines: Turkish, Fast Food
Average price: Under £10
Area: Camden Town, Chalk Farm
Address: 87 Chalk Farm Road
London NW1 8AR
Phone: +44 20 7485 3814

#469
Noorjahan
Cuisines: Indian
Average price: £11-25
Area: Paddington
Address: 26 Sussex Place
London W2 2TH
Phone: +44 20 7402 2332

#470
Byron
Cuisines: American, Burgers
Average price: £11-25
Area: Southwark, Waterloo
Address: 41-45 The Cut
London SE1 8LF
Phone: +44 20 7633 9882

#471
A Fish In A Tie Restaurant
Cuisines: Mediterranean
Average price: Under £10
Area: Battersea
Address: 105 Falcon Road
London SW11 2PF
Phone: +44 20 7924 1913

#472
Portobello Ristorante Pizzeria
Cuisines: Italian, Pizza
Average price: £11-25
Area: Notting Hill
Address: 7 Ladbroke Road
London W11 3PA
Phone: +44 20 7221 1373

#473
Fish Bone
Cuisines: Fish & Chips, British
Average price: Under £10
Area: Fitzrovia
Address: 82 Cleveland Street
London W1T 6NF
Phone: +44 20 7580 2672

#474
Princess Garden Of Mayfair
Cuisines: Chinese
Average price: £11-25
Area: Marylebone
Address: 8-10 N Audley Street
London W1K 6ZD
Phone: +44 20 7493 3223

#475
Brass Rail Salt Beef Bar
Cuisines: Kosher, Sandwiches
Average price: £11-25
Area: Marylebone
Address: 400 Oxford Street
London W1A 1AB

#476
Pizza Metro Pizza
Cuisines: Pizza
Average price: £11-25
Area: Clapham, Clapham Common,
Clapham Junction
Address: 64 Battersea Rise
London SW11 1EQ
Phone: +44 20 7228 3812

#477
Mishkin's
Cuisines: Deli
Average price: £11-25
Area: Covent Garden, Strand
Address: 25 Catherine Street
London WC2B 5JS
Phone: +44 20 7240 2078

#478
Dragon Castle
Cuisines: Chinese
Average price: £11-25
Area: Walworth
Address: 110 Walworth Road
London SE17 1JL
Phone: +44 20 7277 3388

#479
Yashin Sushi Cuisines:
Japanese **Average price:**
Above £46
Area: Kensington
Address: 1A Argyll Road
London W8 7DB
Phone: +44 20 7938 1536

#480
Le Pain Quotidien
Cuisines: Bakery, Breakfast & Brunch,
Coffee & Tea
Average price: £11-25
Area: Notting Hill
Address: 81-85 Notting Hill Gate
London W11 3JS
Phone: +44 20 3657 6938

#481
Tom's Kitchen
Cuisines: British
Average price: £26-45
Area: Chelsea
Address: 27 Cale Street
London SW3 3QP
Phone: +44 20 7349 0202

#482
Simpson's In The Strand
Cuisines: British
Average price: Above £46
Area: Strand
Address: 100 Strand
London WC2R 0EW
Phone: +44 20 7836 9112

#483
Bizzarro Restaurant
Cuisines: Italian
Average price: £11-25
Area: Paddington
Address: 18-22 Craven Road
London W2 3PX
Phone: +44 20 7723 6029

#484
Gay Hussar
Cuisines: Hungarian
Average price: £11-25
Area: Bloomsbury
Address: 2 Greek Street
London W1D 4NB
Phone: +44 20 7437 0973

#485
Wong Kei Restaurant
Cuisines: Chinese
Average price: Under £10
Area: Chinatown
Address: 41-43 Wardour Street
London W1D 6PY
Phone: +44 20 7437 8408

#486
Alain Ducasse at The Dorchester
Cuisines: French
Average price: Above £46
Area: Mayfair
Address: Park Lane
London W1K 1QA
Phone: +44 4402 0762 98866

#487
Androuet
Cuisines: Cheese Shop, Fondue
Average price: £11-25
Area: Brick Lane, Shoreditch, Spitalfields
Address: 107b Commercial Street
London E1 6BG
Phone: +44 20 7375 0642

#488
Bulls Head
Cuisines: Gastropub, Beer, Wine, Spirits
Average price: £11-25
Area: Chiswick, Kew
Address: 15 Strand On the Green
London W4 3PQ
Phone: +44 20 8994 1204

#489
Thai Corner Cafe
Cuisines: Coffee & Tea, Thai
Average price: £11-25
Area: Canonbury, Highbury
Address: 236 St Pauls Road
London N1 2LJ
Phone: +44 20 8299 4041

#490
Yum Bun
Cuisines: Street Vendor, Chinese
Average price: Under £10
Area: Barbican
Address: 31 Featherstone Street
London EC1Y 2BJ
Phone: +44 7919 408221

#491
Apsleys at the Lanesborough
Cuisines: Specialty Food
Average price: Above £46
Area: Belgravia
Address: Hyde Park Corner
London SW1X
Phone: +44 20 7333 7254

#492
Pearl Restaurant & Bar
Cuisines: Bar, European
Average price: Above £46
Area: Holborn
Address: 252 High Holborn
London WC1V 7EN
Phone: +44 20 7829 7000

#493
Patisserie Valerie
Cuisines: Bakery, Cafe
Average price: £11-25
Area: Soho
Address: 44 Old Compton Street
London W1D 4TY
Phone: +44 20 7437 3466

#494
The Camel
Cuisines: Pub, British
Average price: £11-25
Area: Bethnal Green
Address: 277 Globe Rd
London E2 0JD
Phone: +44 20 8981 1448

#495
Byron
Cuisines: Burgers, American
Average price: £11-25
Area: Covent Garden, Strand
Address: 33-35 Wellington Street
London WC2E 7BN
Phone: +44 20 7420 9850

#496
Hawksmoor Guildhall
Cuisines: Steakhouse, Bar, British
Average price: Above £46
Area: The City
Address: 10 Basinghall Street
London EC2V 5BQ
Phone: +44 20 7397 8120

#497
Arigato Japanese Supermarket
Cuisines: Japanese, Grocery
Average price: £11-25
Area: Soho
Address: 48-50 Brewer Street
London W1F 9TG
Phone: +44 20 7287 1722

#498
Needoo Grill
Cuisines: Indian, Pakistani
Average price: £11-25
Area: Whitechapel
Address: 87 New Road
London E1 1HH
Phone: +44 20 7247 0648

#499
El Pirata De Tapas
Cuisines: Spanish, Tapas Bar
Average price: £11-25
Area: Bayswater
Address: 115 Westbourne Grove
London W2 4UP
Phone: +44 20 7727 5000

#500
Daphne's
Cuisines: Italian
Average price: Above £46
Area: Chelsea
Address: 112 Draycott Avenue
London SW3 3AE
Phone: +44 20 7589 4257

#501
The Lyric
Cuisines: British, Pub, American
Average price: £11-25
Area: Soho
Address: 37 Great Windmill Street
London W1D 7LT
Phone: +44 20 7434 0604

#502
Edo
Cuisines: Japanese
Average price: £26-45
Area: Norwood (West & Upper)
Address: 18 Westow Hill
London SE19 1RX
Phone: +44 20 8670 8900

#503
19 Numara Bos Cirrik 1
Cuisines: Turkish
Average price: £11-25
Area: Dalston
Address: 34 Stoke Newington Road
London N16 7XJ
Phone: +44 20 7249 0400

#504
Mandalay Burmese Restaurant
Cuisines: Burmese
Average price: Under £10
Area: Lisson Grove
Address: 444 Edgware Road
London W2 1EG
Phone: +44 20 7258 3696

#505
Charlotte Street Hotel
Cuisines: Hotel, European, Lounge
Average price: £26-45
Area: Fitzrovia
Address: 15-17 Charlotte Street
London W1T 1RJ
Phone: +44 20 7806 2000

#506
Soho Kitchen and Bar
Cuisines: Diner
Average price: £11-25
Area: Bloomsbury
Address: 19-21 Old Compton Street
London W1D 5JJ
Phone: +44 20 7734 5656

#507
Il Bordello
Cuisines: Pizza, Italian
Average price: £11-25
Area: Wapping
Address: 81 Wapping High Street
London E1W 2YN
Phone: +44 20 7481 9950

#508
Four O Nine
Cuisines: European
Average price: £26-45
Area: Clapham
Address: 409 Clapham Road
London SW9 9BT
Phone: +44 20 7737 0722

#509
Tajima-Tei Cuisines:
Japanese **Average
price:** £11-25
Area: Farringdon
Address: 9-15 Leather Lane Unit 1
London EC1N 7ST
Phone: +44 20 7404 9665

#510
Wagamama
Cuisines: Japanese, Asian Fusion
Average price: £11-25
Area: South Bank, Southwark
Address: Royal Festival Hall
London SE1 8XX
Phone: +44 20 7021 0877

#511
Pizza East
Cuisines: Pizza
Average price: £11-25
Area: Shoreditch
Address: 56 Shoreditch High Street
London E1 6JJ
Phone: +44 20 7729 1888

#512
Café Boheme
Cuisines: French, Cafe
Average price: £11-25
Area: Bloomsbury
Address: 13 Old Compton Street
London W1D 5JQ
Phone: +44 20 7734 0623

#513
Balans
Cuisines: Breakfast & Brunch
Average price: £11-25
Area: Kensington
Address: 187 Kensington High Street
London W8 6SH
Phone: +44 20 7376 0115

#514
Taste Of Siam
Cuisines: Thai
Average price: Under £10
Area: Euston, Camden Town
Address: 45 Camden High Street
London NW1 7JH
Phone: +44 20 7380 0665

#515
Vanilla Black
Cuisines: Vegetarian
Average price: £26-45
Area: Holborn
Address: 17-18 Took's Court
London EC4A 1LB
Phone: +44 20 7242 2622

#516
Pieminister
Cuisines: British
Average price: Under £10
Area: Southwark
Address: 56 Upper Ground
London SE1 9PP
Phone: +44 20 7928 5755

#517
Bonda Cafe
Cuisines: Malaysian
Average price: Under £10
Area: Paddington
Address: 190 Sussex Garden
London W2 1TU
Phone: +44 20 7402 5111

#518
Murano
Cuisines: Italian
Average price: Above £46
Area: Mayfair
Address: 20 Queen Street
London W1J 5PP
Phone: +44 20 7495 1127

#519
Rabieng Thai Restaurant
Cuisines: Thai
Average price: £11-25
Area: Islington
Address: 143 Upper Street
London N1 1QY
Phone: +44 20 7226 2014

#520
Bamboula
Cuisines: Caribbean, Ethnic Food,
Fast Food
Average price: £11-25
Area: Stockwell
Address: 12 Acre Lane
London SW2 5SG
Phone: +44 20 7737 6633

#521
On The Bab
Cuisines: Korean
Average price: £11-25
Area: Hoxton, Hoxton Square
Address: 305 Old Street
London EC1V 9LA
Phone: +44 20 7683 0361

#522
Real Ale Taproom
Cuisines: Gastropub, Pub
Average price: £11-25
Area: Islington
Address: 163 Upper Street
London N1 1HU
Phone: +44 20 7288 1606

#523
28-50
Cuisines: Wine Bar, French
Average price: £26-45
Area: Holborn
Address: 140 Fetter Lane
London EC4A 1BT
Phone: +44 20 7242 8877

#524
Browns Restaurant
Cuisines: British
Average price: £26-45
Area: Marylebone, Piccadilly
Address: 47 Maddox Street
London W1S 2PG
Phone: +44 20 7491 4565

#525
Sông Quê
Cuisines: Vietnamese
Average price: £11-25
Area: Haggerston
Address: 134 Kingsland Road
London E2 8DY
Phone: +44 20 7613 3222

#526
Afghan Kitchen
Cuisines: Afghan
Average price: £11-25
Area: Angel, Islington
Address: 35 Islington Green
London N1 8DU
Phone: +44 20 7359 8019

#527
French House
Cuisines: European, Pub, British
Average price: £11-25
Area: Soho
Address: 49 Dean Street
London W1D 5BG
Phone: +44 20 7437 2477

#528
Mien Tay
Cuisines: Vietnamese
Average price: Under £10
Area: Shoreditch
Address: 122 Kingsland Road
London E2 8DP
Phone: +44 20 7729 3074

#529
Paolina's Thai Cafe
Cuisines: Coffee & Tea, Thai
Average price: Under £10
Area: Bloomsbury
Address: 181 King's Cross Road
London WC1X 9BZ
Phone: +44 20 7278 8176

#530
The Roastery Cafe
Cuisines: Cafe
Average price: Under £10
Area: Clapham
Address: 789 Wandsworth Road
London SW8 3JQ
Phone: +44 20 7350 1961

#531
Franco's Take Away
Cuisines: Fast Food, Italian
Average price: £26-45
Area: Hoxton
Address: 67 Rivington Street
London EC2A 3AY
Phone: +44 20 7739 0231

#532
Dulwich Picture Gallery
Cuisines: Art Gallery, Cafe
Average price: Under £10
Area: Dulwich
Address: Gallery Road
London SE21 7AD
Phone: +44 20 8693 5254

#533
Wright Brothers
Cuisines: Seafood
Average price: £26-45
Area: Soho
Address: 13 Kingly Street
London W1B 5PW
Phone: +44 20 7434 3611

#534
Jamie's Italian
Cuisines: Italian
Average price: £11-25
Area: Covent Garden
Address: 11 Upper St Martin's Lane
London WC2H 9FB
Phone: +44 20 3326 6390

#535
Dehesa
Cuisines: Spanish, Basque
Average price: £26-45
Area: Soho
Address: 25 Ganton Street
London W1F 9BP
Phone: +44 20 7494 4170

#536
Patisserie Valerie
Cuisines: French, Bakery, Desserts, Cafe,
Coffee & Tea
Average price: £11-25
Area: Marylebone
Address: 105 Marylebone High Road
London W1U 4RS
Phone: +44 20 7935 6240

#537
Morito
Cuisines: Tapas, Spanish
Average price: £11-25
Area: Clerkenwell
Address: 32 Exmouth Market
London EC1R 4QE
Phone: +44 20 7278 7007

#538
Burger & Lobster
Cuisines: American, Burgers, Seafood
Average price: £11-25
Area: Farringdon
Address: 40 Saint John's Street
London EC1M 4AY
Phone: +44 20 7490 9230

#539
Wafflemeister
Cuisines: Desserts, Ice Cream, Belgian
Average price: Under £10
Area: South Kensington
Address: 26 Cromwell Place
London SW7 2DL
Phone: +44 20 7193 8649

#540
Kettner's
Cuisines: European, Champagne Bar
Average price: £26-45
Area: Bloomsbury **Address:**
29 Romilly Street London
W1D 5HP
Phone: +44 20 7734 6112

#541
Plateau Restaurant
Cuisines: Bar, British, French, European,
Burgers
Average price: £26-45
Area: Canary Wharf, Isle of Dogs
Address: Canada Place
London E14 5ER
Phone: +44 20 7715 7100

#542
Brasserie Zédel
Cuisines: Brasserie, Jazz & Blues,
Cocktail Bar
Average price: £11-25
Area: Soho
Address: 20 Sherwood Street
London W1F 7ED
Phone: +44 20 7734 4888

#543
Durum Restaurant
Cuisines: Turkish
Average price: £11-25
Area: Finchley
Address: 119 Ballards Lane
London N3 1LJ
Phone: +44 20 8346 8977

#544
Rochelle Canteen
Cuisines: Caterers, British
Average price: £11-25
Area: Shoreditch, Bethnal Green
Address: School House
London E2 7ES
Phone: +44 20 7729 5677

#545
The Queen of Sheba
Cuisines: Ethiopian, African
Average price: £11-25
Area: Kentish Town
Address: 12 Fortess Road
London NW5 2EU
Phone: +44 20 7284 3947

#546
The Gallery
Cuisines: British, Bar
Average price: £26-45
Area: West Hampstead
Address: 190 Broadhurst Gardens
London NW6 3AY
Phone: +44 20 7625 9184

#547
The Greedy Buddha
Cuisines: Indian, Asian Fusion
Average price: £11-25
Area: Fulham
Address: 144 Wandsworth Bridge Road
London SW6 2UH
Phone: +44 20 7751 3311

#548
Sömine
Cuisines: Turkish
Average price: Under £10
Area: De Beauvoir, Kingsland
Address: 131 Kingsland High Street
London E8 2PB
Phone: +44 20 7254 7384

#549
Little Bay Restaurant
Cuisines: Mediterranean,
French, European
Average price: £11-25
Area: Bloomsbury
Address: 171 Farringdon Road
London EC1R 3AL
Phone: +44 20 7278 1234

#550
Builders Arms
Cuisines: Pub, British
Average price: £11-25
Area: Kensington
Address: 1 Kensington Court Place
London W8 5BJ
Phone: +44 20 7937 6213

#551
Grumbles
Cuisines: British, French
Average price: £11-25
Area: Pimlico
Address: 35 Churton Street
London SW1V 2LT
Phone: +44 20 7834 0149

#552
Busaba Eathai
Cuisines: Thai
Average price: £11-25
Area: Bloomsbury
Address: 22 Store Street
London WC1E 7DF
Phone: +44 20 7299 7900

#553
Blandfords Café
Cuisines: Coffee & Tea, Italian, Pizza
Average price: Under £10
Area: Marylebone
Address: 65 Chiltern Street
London W1U 6NH
Phone: +44 20 7486 4117

#554
Raj Of India
Cuisines: Indian, Pakistani
Average price: £11-25
Area: West Kensington
Address: 46 Shepherds Bush Road
London W6 7PJ
Phone: +44 20 7602 9930

#555
Firezza
Cuisines: Pizza
Average price: £11-25
Area: Canonbury, Highbury
Address: 276 St Pauls Road
London N1 2LH
Phone: +44 20 7359 7400

#556
Gaucho
Cuisines: Argentine, Steakhouse
Average price: £26-45
Area: Hampstead Village
Address: 64 Heath Street
London NW3 1DN
Phone: +44 20 7431 8222

#557
Les Deux Salons
Cuisines: French
Average price: £26-45
Area: Covent Garden, Strand
Address: 40 - 42 William IV Street
London WC2N 4DD
Phone: +44 20 7420 2050

#558
Inhabition Coffee Shop
Cuisines: Coffee & Tea, Diner
Average price: £11-25
Area: Camden Town
Address: 15 Chalk Farm Road
London NW1 8AG
Phone: +44 20 7485 1440

#559
Rivington Grill
Cuisines: British
Average price: £26-45
Area: Hoxton
Address: 28-30 Rivington Street
London EC2A 3DZ
Phone: +44 20 7729 7053

#560
Nando's
Cuisines: Portuguese, Chicken Wings
Average price: £11-25
Area: South Kensington
Address: 117 Gloucester Road
London SW7 4ST
Phone: +44 20 7373 4446

#561
Bumpkin Notting Hill
Cuisines: British, Breakfast & Brunch
Average price: £11-25
Area: Notting Hill
Address: 209 Westbourne Park Road
London W11 1EA
Phone: +44 20 7243 9818

#562
Pierino Pizza Pasta
Cuisines: Pizza, Italian
Average price: £11-25
Area: South Kensington
Address: 37 Thurloe Place
London SW7 2HP
Phone: +44 20 7581 3770

#563
Tas Firin Restaurant
Cuisines: Turkish
Average price: £11-25
Area: Brick Lane, Shoreditch
Address: 160 Bethnal Green Road
London E2 6DG
Phone: +44 20 7729 6446

#564
Bar Du Marché
Cuisines: Wine Bar, French
Average price: £11-25
Area: Soho
Address: 19 Berwick Street
London W1F 0PX
Phone: +44 20 7734 4606

#565
Pizza Express
Cuisines: Pizza, Italian
Average price: £11-25
Area: Soho
Address: 10 Dean Street
London W1D 3RW
Phone: +44 20 7437 9595

#566
Namaaste Kitchen
Cuisines: Indian
Average price: £26-45
Area: Camden Town
Address: 64 Parkway
London NW1 7AH
Phone: +44 20 7485 5977

#567
Jasmine
Cuisines: Thai
Average price: £11-25
Area: Shepherd's Bush
Address: 16 Goldhawk Road
London W12 8DH
Phone: +44 20 8743 7920

#568
The Lost Angel
Cuisines: Bar, Steakhouse
Average price: £11-25
Area: Battersea
Address: 339 Battersea Park Road
London SW11 4LS
Phone: +44 20 7622 2112

#569
Whits
Cuisines: French
Average price: £26-45
Area: Kensington
Address: 21 Abingdon Road
London W8 6AH
Phone: +44 20 7938 1122

#570
Boot and Flogger
Cuisines: Wine Bar, British
Average price: £11-25
Area: Borough
Address: 10-20 Redcross Way
London SE1 1TA
Phone: +44 20 7407 1116

#571
Floridita
Cuisines: Cuban, Lounge,
Latin American
Average price: £11-25
Area: Soho
Address: 100 Wardour Street
London W1F 0TN
Phone: +44 20 7314 4000

#572
Patara
Cuisines: Thai
Average price: £26-45
Area: Marylebone, Piccadilly
Address: 7 Maddox Street
London W1S 2QB
Phone: +44 20 7499 6008

#573
Coq D'Argent
Cuisines: French
Average price: £26-45
Area: The City
Address: 1 Poultry
London EC2R 8EJ
Phone: +44 20 7395 5000

#574
The Greenhouse
Cuisines: French, European, British
Average price: Above £46
Area: Mayfair
Address: 27a Hay's Mews
London W1J 5NY
Phone: +44 20 7499 3331

#575
Goodman
Cuisines: Steakhouse
Average price: £26-45
Area: Isle of Dogs, Millwall
Address: 3 South Quay
London E14 9RU
Phone: +44 20 7531 0300

#576
Soho Joe
Cuisines: Pizza, Coffee & Tea
Average price: Under £10
Area: Soho
Address: 22-25 Dean Street
London W1D 3RY
Phone: +44 7534 134398

#577
Taro Restaurant
Cuisines: Japanese, Sushi Bar
Average price: £11-25
Area: Soho
Address: 61 Brewer Street
London W1F 0RB
Phone: +44 20 7734 5826

#578
Nagomi
Cuisines: Japanese
Average price: £11-25
Area: Marylebone
Address: 4 Blenheim Street
London W1S 1LB
Phone: +44 20 7165 9506

#579
Mamuśka!
Cuisines: Polish
Average price: Under £10
Area: Elephant & Castle, Newington
Address: 1st Floor Unit 233
London SE1 6TE
Phone: +44 20 3602 1898

#580
Tukdin Flavours of Malaysia
Cuisines: Malaysian
Average price: £11-25
Area: Bayswater
Address: 41 Craven Road
London W2 3BX
Phone: +44 20 7723 6955

#581
Noura
Cuisines: Middle Eastern, Vegetarian
Average price: £26-45
Area: Belgravia
Address: 16 Hobart Place
London SW1W 0HH
Phone: +44 20 7235 9444

#582
Crème de la Crêpe
Cuisines: Creperie, Desserts
Average price: Under £10
Area: Covent Garden, Strand
Address: 29 The Piazza
London WC2E 8RE
Phone: +44 20 7836 6896

#583
Paul
Cuisines: Bakery, French
Average price: Under £10
Area: Chelsea, Knightsbridge
Address: 122 Brompton Road
London SW3 1JD
Phone: +44 20 7584 6117

#584
Bonnington Café
Cuisines: Vegetarian, Vegan
Average price: Under £10
Area: Oval, South Lambeth, Vauxhall,
Kennington
Address: 11 Vauxhall Grove
London SW8 1TD

#585
The Wells
Cuisines: Wine Bar, Pub, British
Average price: £11-25
Area: Hampstead Village
Address: 30 Well Walk
London NW3 1BX
Phone: +44 20 7794 3785

#586
Gaucho
Cuisines: Argentine, Steakhouse
Average price: £26-45
Area: The City
Address: 1 Bell Inn Yard
London EC3V 0BL
Phone: +44 20 7626 5180

#587
Magdalen
Cuisines: British, French
Average price: £26-45
Area: London Bridge
Address: 152 Tooley Street
London SE1 2TU
Phone: +44 20 7403 1342

#588
M1LK
Cuisines: Coffee & Tea,
Breakfast & Brunch
Average price: £11-25
Area: Balham
Address: 20 Bedford Hill
London SW12 9RG
Phone: +44 4420 8772 9085

#589
Tagine Restaurant
Cuisines: Moroccan
Average price: £11-25
Area: Balham
Address: 1-3 Fernlea Road
London SW12 9RT
Phone: +44 20 8675 7604

#590
Les Trois Garcons
Cuisines: French
Average price: Above £46
Area: Brick Lane, Shoreditch,
Bethnal Green
Address: 1 Club Row
London E1 6JX
Phone: +44 20 7613 1924

#591
Sam's Brasserie & Bar
Cuisines: Breakfast & Brunch,
British, Brasserie
Average price: £26-45
Area: Chiswick
Address: 11 Barley Mow Passage
London W4 4PH
Phone: +44 20 8987 0555

#592
Haché
Cuisines: Burgers
Average price: £11-25
Area: Chelsea
Address: 329-331 Fulham Road
London SW10 9QL
Phone: +44 20 7823 3515

#593
Ping Pong Cuisines:
Dim Sum **Average**
price: £11-25
Area: Soho
Address: 45 Great Marlborough Street
London W1F 7JL
Phone: +44 20 7851 6969

#594
Roast
Cuisines: British
Average price: £26-45
Area: London Bridge
Address: Stoney Street
London SE1 1TL
Phone: +44 845 034 7300

#595
Cafe Pacifico
Cuisines: Mexican, Bar
Average price: £11-25
Area: Covent Garden
Address: 5 Langley Street
London WC2H 9JA
Phone: +44 20 7379 7728

#596
Indian Veg Bhelpoori House
Cuisines: Indian, Vegetarian
Average price: Under £10
Area: Islington
Address: 92-93 Chapel Market
London N1 9EX
Phone: +44 20 7833 1167

#597
Mela
Cuisines: Indian, Pakistani
Average price: £11-25
Area: Covent Garden
Address: 152-156 Shaftesbury Avenue
London WC2H 8HL
Phone: +44 20 7836 8635

#598
YouMeSushi
Cuisines: Food Delivery Service,
Japanese, Sushi Bar
Average price: £11-25
Area: Fitzrovia
Address: 37 Tottenham Court Road
London W1T 1BY
Phone: +44 20 7323 2266

#599
The Harrison
Cuisines: Gastropub, British,
Bed & Breakfast
Average price: £11-25
Area: Bloomsbury
Address: 28 Harrison Street
London WC1H 8JF
Phone: +44 20 7278 3966

#600
Shake Shack
Cuisines: Burgers
Average price: £11-25
Area: Covent Garden, Strand
Address: 24 Market Building
London WC2E 8RD
Phone: +44 20 3598 1360

#601
Fire & Stone
Cuisines: Pizza
Average price: £11-25
Area: Covent Garden, Strand
Address: 31/32 Maiden Lane
London WC2E 7JS
Phone: +44 844 371 2550

#602
Fork Deli Patisserie
Cuisines: Cafe, Coffee & Tea
Average price: Under £10
Area: Bloomsbury
Address: 85 Marchmont Street
London WC1N 1AL

#603
Zeitgeist
Cuisines: German
Average price: £11-25
Area: Vauxhall, Southwark
Address: 49 - 51 Black Prince Road
London SE11 6AB
Phone: +44 20 7840 0426

#604
Taquería Cuisines:
Mexican **Average**
price: £11-25
Area: Notting Hill
Address: 139-143 Westbourne Grove
London W11 2RS
Phone: +44 20 7229 4734

#605
Nandos
Cuisines: Portuguese, Chicken Wings
Average price: £11-25
Area: Earls Court, South Kensington
Address: 204 Earls Court Road
London SW5 9QF
Phone: +44 20 7259 2544

#606
Applebee's Fish Shop & Café
Cuisines: Seafood
Average price: £11-25
Area: London Bridge
Address: 5 Stoney Street
London SE1 9AA
Phone: +44 20 7407 5777

#607
Trader Vic's
Cuisines: Hawaiian, Cocktail Bar
Average price: £26-45
Area: Mayfair
Address: 22 Park Lane
London W1K 1BE
Phone: +44 20 7208 4113

#608
Euphorium Bakery
Cuisines: Coffee & Tea, Bakery, Breakfast
& Brunch
Average price: Under £10
Area: Angel, Islington
Address: 79 Upper Street
London N1 0NU
Phone: +44 20 7288 8788

#609
Beirut Express
Cuisines: Middle Eastern, Fast Food
Average price: Under £10
Area: Marylebone
Address: 112 Edgware Road
London W2 2DZ
Phone: +44 20 7724 2700

#610
La Bouchee
Cuisines: French
Average price: £26-45
Area: South Kensington
Address: 56 Old Brompton Road
London SW7 3DY
Phone: +44 20 7589 1929

#611
Busaba Eathai
Cuisines: Thai
Average price: £11-25
Area: Marylebone
Address: 8-13 Bird Street
London W1U 1BU
Phone: +44 20 7518 8080

#612
The Queen's Arms
Cuisines: Pub, British
Average price: £11-25
Area: Knightsbridge
Address: 30 Queen's Gate Mews
London SW7 5QL
Phone: +44 20 7823 9293

#613
The Shed
Cuisines: British
Average price: £26-45
Area: Notting Hill
Address: 122 Palace Gardens Terrace
London W8 4RT
Phone: +44 20 7229 4024

#614
Maggie's Cafe & Restaurant
Cuisines: British
Average price: Under £10
Area: Lewisham
Address: 322 Lewisham Rd
London SE13 7PA
Phone: +44 20 8244 0339

#615
Entrée Restaurant & Bar
Cuisines: European
Average price: £26-45
Area: Clapham, Clapham Common,
Clapham Junction
Address: 2 Battersea Rise
London SW11 1ED
Phone: +44 20 7223 5147

#616
Taiwan Village
Cuisines: Taiwanese, Chinese
Average price: £11-25
Area: West Kensington, Earls Court, West
Brompton
Address: 85 Lillie Road
London SW6 1UD
Phone: +44 20 7381 2900

#617
Bodean's Cuisines:
American **Average
price:** £11-25
Area: Clapham Common
Address: 169 Clapham High Street
London SW4 7SS
Phone: +44 20 7622 4248

#618
Sichuan Folk
Cuisines: Chinese
Average price: £11-25
Area: Brick Lane, Shoreditch
Address: 32 Hanbury Street
London E1 6QR
Phone: +44 20 7247 4735

#619
Sartori
Cuisines: Pizza
Average price: £11-25
Area: Covent Garden
Address: 16 Great Newport Street
London WC2H 7JE
Phone: +44 20 7836 6308

#620
Palm Court at The Langham Hotel
Cuisines: Coffee & Tea, Restaurant
Average price: £26-45
Area: Marylebone
Address: 1C Portland Place
London W1B 1JA
Phone: +44 20 7965 0195

#621
Oliveto
Cuisines: Italian
Average price: £11-25
Area: Belgravia
Address: 49 Elizabeth Street
London SW1W 9PP
Phone: +44 20 7730 0074

#622
Barbecoa
Cuisines: Barbeque, Butcher
Average price: Above £46
Area: Blackfriars, The City
Address: 20 New Change Passage
London EC4M 9AG
Phone: +44 20 3005 8555

#623
Spices Cuisines:
Indian **Average price:**
£11-25
Area: Islington
Address: 10 Chapel Market
London N1 9EZ
Phone: +44 20 7837 7151

#624
Garufa
Cuisines: Argentine, Breakfast & Brunch
Average price: £11-25
Area: Highbury
Address: 104 Highbury Park
London N5 2XE
Phone: +44 20 7226 0070

#625
Donna Margherita
Cuisines: Italian, Pizza
Average price: £26-45
Area: Clapham
Address: 183 Lavender Hill
London SW11 5TE
Phone: +44 20 7228 2660

#626
Thai Taste
Cuisines: Thai
Average price: £26-45
Area: South Kensington
Address: 130 Cromwell Road
London SW7 4ET
Phone: +44 20 7373 1647

#627
Herman Ze German
Cuisines: German, Hot Dogs
Average price: Under £10
Area: Strand
Address: 19 Villiers Street
London WC2N 6NE
Phone: +44 20 7930 4827

#628
Bill's
Cuisines: Breakfast & Brunch, European,
British
Average price: £11-25
Area: Soho
Address: 36-44 Brewer Street
London W1F 9TB
Phone: +44 20 7287 8712

#629
Candy Café
Cuisines: Chinese, Cafe, Desserts
Average price: Under £10
Area: Chinatown
Address: 3 Macclesfield Street
London W1D 6AU
Phone: +44 20 7434 4581

#630
Beach Blanket Babylon
Cuisines: Lounge, European,
Cocktail Bar
Average price: £26-45
Area: Notting Hill
Address: 45 Ledbury Road
London W11 2AA
Phone: +44 20 7229 2907

#631
Gaby's
Cuisines: Deli
Average price: £11-25
Area: Covent Garden, Strand
Address: 30 Charing Cross Road
London WC2H 0DB
Phone: +44 20 7836 4233

#632
**Gilgamesh Restaurant
Bar & Lounge**
Cuisines: Asian Fusion,
Lounge, Middle Eastern
Average price: £26-45
Area: Camden Town
Address: Chalk Farm Road
London NW1 8AH
Phone: +44 20 7428 4922

#633
Yum Yum
Cuisines: Thai
Average price: £11-25
Area: Stoke Newington Central
Address: 187 Stoke Newington High
Street, London N16 0LH
Phone: +44 20 7254 6751

#634
Ceviche Cuisines:
Peruvian **Average
price:** £26-45
Area: Soho
Address: 17 Frith Street
London W1D 4RG
Phone: +44 20 7292 2040

#635
Negozio Classica
Cuisines: Italian, Wine Bar
Average price: £11-25
Area: Notting Hill
Address: 283 Westbourne Grove
London W11 2QA
Phone: +44 20 7034 0005

#636
Thai Corner Cafe
Cuisines: Thai
Average price: £11-25
Area: Peckham Rye
Address: 44 N Cross Road
London SE22 9EU
Phone: +44 20 8299 4041

#637
Long White Cloud
Cuisines: Cafe, Coffee & Tea
Average price: £11-25
Area: Haggerston
Address: 151 Hackney Road
London E2 8JL
Phone: +44 20 7033 4642

#638
Le Vacherin
Cuisines: French
Average price: £26-45
Area: South Acton
Address: 76-77 S Parade
London W4 5LF
Phone: +44 20 8742 2121

#639
Park Room and Library
Cuisines: Coffee & Tea, British
Average price: £26-45
Area: Mayfair
Address: 86-90 Park Lane
London W1K 7TN
Phone: +44 4420 7499 6363

#640
Indian City
Cuisines: Indian
Average price: £11-25
Area: Blackfriars, Holborn
Address: 4 New Bridge Street
London EC4V 6AA
Phone: +44 20 7583 4673

#641
Sardo Cuisines:
Italian **Average price:**
£26-45
Area: Fitzrovia
Address: 45 Grafton Way
London W1T 5DQ
Phone: +44 20 7387 2521

#642
Mortimer & Bennett
Cuisines: Deli, Specialty Food
Area: Chiswick
Address: 34 Turnham Green Terrace
London W4 1RG
Phone: +44 20 8995 4145

#643
Ziani Restaurant
Cuisines: Italian
Average price: £26-45
Area: Chelsea
Address: 45 Radnor Walk
London SW3 4BP
Phone: +44 20 7352 2698

#644
Browns of Brockley
Cuisines: Cafe, Coffee & Tea
Average price: £11-25
Area: Brockley
Address: 5 Coulgate Street
London SE4 2RW
Phone: +44 20 8692 0722

#645
Bengal Restaurant
Cuisines: Indian, Food Delivery Service
Average price: £11-25
Area: Bayswater
Address: 62a Porchester Road
London W2 6ET
Phone: +44 20 7229 5567

#646
Inamo
Cuisines: Asian Fusion
Average price: £26-45
Area: Soho
Address: 134-136 Wardour Street
London W1F 8ZP
Phone: +44 20 7851 7051

#647
Lantana
Cuisines: Breakfast & Brunch, Cafe
Average price: £11-25
Area: Fitzrovia
Address: 13 Charlotte Place
London W1T 1SN
Phone: +44 20 7637 3347

#648
Saigon Saigon
Cuisines: Vietnamese
Average price: £11-25
Area: Hammersmith
Address: 313-317 King Street
London W6 9NH
Phone: +44 20 8748 6887

#649
Ravi Shankar
Cuisines: Indian, Vegetarian, Pakistani
Average price: Under £10
Area: Euston
Address: 133-135 Drummond Street
London NW1 2HL
Phone: +44 20 7388 6458

#650
Frontline Restaurant
Cuisines: British
Average price: £26-45
Area: Paddington
Address: 13 Norfolk Place
London W2 1QJ
Phone: +44 20 7479 8960

#651
Lock 7
Cuisines: Deli, Bike Rentals,
Coffee & Tea
Average price: £26-45
Area: Bethnal Green
Address: 129 Pritchards Road
London E2 9AP
Phone: +44 20 7739 3042

#652
Pix
Cuisines: Tapas Bar, Lounge
Average price: £11-25
Area: Covent Garden
Address: 63 Neal Street
London WC2H 9PJ
Phone: +44 20 7836 9779

#653
Skylon
Cuisines: European, British
Average price: £26-45
Area: South Bank, Southwark
Address: Belvedere Road
London SE1 8XX
Phone: +44 20 7654 7800

#654
Joanna's
Cuisines: European, Breakfast & Brunch
Average price: £26-45
Area: Norwood (West & Upper)
Address: 56 Westow Hill
London SE19 1RX
Phone: +44 20 8670 4052

#655
The Engineer
Cuisines: Pub, British
Average price: £26-45
Area: Camden Town, Primrose Hill
Address: 65 Gloucester Avenue
London NW1 8JH
Phone: +44 20 7483 1890

#656
Sagar
Cuisines: Vegetarian, Indian, Vegan
Average price: £11-25
Area: Hammersmith
Address: 157 King Street
London W6 9JT
Phone: +44 20 8741 8563

#657
The Green Man
Cuisines: Pub, British
Average price: £11-25
Area: Fitzrovia
Address: 36 Riding House Street
London W1W 7EP
Phone: +44 20 7580 9087

#658
Rosa's Spitalfields
Cuisines: Thai
Average price: £11-25
Area: Brick Lane, Shoreditch
Address: 12 Hanbury Street
London E1 6QR
Phone: +44 20 7247 1093

#659
Cyprus Mangal
Cuisines: Turkish
Average price: £11-25
Area: Victoria
Address: 45 Warwick Way
London SW1V 1QS
Phone: +44 20 7828 5940

#660
Danny's Gourmet Wraps
Cuisines: Cafe, Juice Bar
Average price: Under £10
Area: Bloomsbury
Address: 31 Lambs Conduit Street
London WC1N 3NG
Phone: +44 20 7404 5128

#661
Albertini Cafe
Cuisines: Cafe
Average price: Under £10
Area: Euston
Address: 16-20 Chalton Street
London NW1 1JH
Phone: +44 20 7387 4723

#662
19 Numara Bos Cirrik 2
Cuisines: Turkish
Area: Stoke Newington Central
Address: 194 Stoke Newington High St
London N16 7JD
Phone: +44 20 7249 9111

#663
Hala Restaurant
Cuisines: Turkish
Average price: Under £10
Area: Noel Park, Turnpike Lane,
Wood Green
Address: 29 Green Parade
London N4 1LG
Phone: +44 20 8802 4883

#664
The Northall Restaurant
The Corinthia Hotel London
Cuisines: European
Average price: £26-45
Area: Westminster
Address: Whitehall Place
London SW1A 2BD

#665
Côte Brasserie
Cuisines: French, Brasserie,
Breakfast & Brunch
Average price: £26-45
Area: Chiswick
Address: 50-54 Turnham Green Terrace
London W4 1QP
Phone: +44 20 8747 6788

#666
Pret A Manger
Cuisines: Coffee & Tea, Sandwiches
Area: Fitzrovia
Address: 136 Great Portland Street
London W1W 6PY
Phone: +44 20 7932 5340

#667
Kokeb Ethiopian Cuisine
Cuisines: Ethiopian
Average price: £11-25
Area: Barnsbury, Lower Holloway
Address: 45 Roman Way
London N7 8XF
Phone: +44 20 7609 9832

#668
Brasserie Max
Cuisines: European
Average price: £26-45
Area: Covent Garden
Address: 8 Monmouth Street
London WC2H 9HB
Phone: +44 20 7806 1000

#669
TGI Fridays UK
Cuisines: American
Average price: £11-25
Area: Kingston Upon Thames
Address: Wood Street Kingston Upon
Thames KT1 1TR
Phone: +44 20 8547 2900

#670
Café Kick
Cuisines: Pub, Coffee & Tea, Tapas
Average price: £11-25
Area: Clerkenwell
Address: 43 Exmouth Market
London EC1R 4QL
Phone: +44 20 7837 8077

#671
Lowlander
Cuisines: Pub, Belgian
Average price: £11-25
Area: Covent Garden
Address: 36 Drury Lane
London WC2B 5RR
Phone: +44 20 7379 7446

#672
Pizza Express
Cuisines: Pizza, Italian
Average price: £11-25
Area: Strand
Address: 450 Strand
London WC2R 0RG
Phone: +44 20 7930 8205

#673
Yumchaa
Cuisines: Coffee & Tea,
Cafe, Tea Room
Average price: Under £10
Area: Camden Town
Address: 91-92 Camden Lock Place
London NW1 8AF
Phone: +44 20 7209 9641

#674
Antonio's Ristorante
Cuisines: Italian
Average price: £11-25
Area: Angel, Islington
Address: Rear of 137 Upper Street
London N1 1QP
Phone: +44 20 7226 8994

#675
St John's Tavern
Cuisines: Gastropub, Pub
Average price: £26-45
Area: Tufnell Park, Upper Holloway
Address: 91 Junction Road
London N19 5QU
Phone: +44 20 7272 1587

#676
Cubana Bar - Restaurant
Cuisines: Latin American
Average price: £11-25
Area: Southwark, Waterloo
Address: 48 Lower Marsh
London SE1 7RG
Phone: +44 20 7928 8778

#677
Riding House Café
Cuisines: Tapas, British
Average price: £11-25
Area: Fitzrovia
Address: 43-51 Great Tichfield Street
London W1W 7PQ
Phone: +44 20 7927 0840

#678
Mouse & de Lotz
Cuisines: British
Average price: Under £10
Area: Dalston
Address: 103 Shacklewell Lane
London E8 2AB
Phone: +44 20 3489 8082

#679
Giacobazzi's Delicatessen
Cuisines: Deli, Caterers, Beer,
Wine, Spirits
Average price: £11-25
Area: Hampstead Heath
Address: 150 Fleet Road
London NW3 2QX
Phone: +44 20 7267 7222

#680
Skipjacks
Cuisines: Seafood, Fish & Chips
Average price: £11-25
Area: Harrow & Wealdstone
Address: 268-276 Streatfield Road Harrow
HA3 9BY
Phone: +44 20 8204 9391

#681
Kennington Lane Cafe
Cuisines: Cafe
Average price: Under £10
Area: Oval, South Lambeth, Vauxhall
Address: 383 Kennington Lane
London SE11 5QY
Phone: +44 20 7735 5853

#682
Bageriet
Cuisines: Scandinavian, Bakery
Average price: Under £10
Area: Covent Garden
Address: 24 Rose Street
London WC2E 9EA
Phone: +44 20 7240 0000

#683
Chilango
Cuisines: Mexican
Average price: Under £10
Area: Blackfriars, Holborn
Address: 142 Fleet Street
London EC4A 2BP
Phone: +44 20 7353 6761

#684
Wagamama
Cuisines: Japanese, Asian Fusion
Average price: £11-25
Area: Chelsea
Address: 109-125 Brompton Road
London SW1X 7RJ
Phone: +44 20 7201 8000

#685
Pearl Liang
Cuisines: Dim Sum
Average price: £11-25
Area: Paddington
Address: 8 Sheldon Square
London W2 6EZ
Phone: +44 20 7289 7000

#686
The Junction Tavern
Cuisines: Pub, Gastropub
Average price: £11-25
Area: Kentish Town
Address: 101 Fortess Road
London NW5 1AG
Phone: +44 20 7485 9400

#687
The Wet Fish Café & Brasserie
Cuisines: British, Brasserie
Average price: £11-25
Area: West Hampstead
Address: 242 West End Lane
London NW6 1LG
Phone: +44 20 7443 9222

#688
Roka
Cuisines: Japanese, Sushi Bar
Average price: £26-45
Area: Canary Wharf, Isle of Dogs
Address: 40 Canada Square
London E14 5FW
Phone: +44 852 3960 5988

#689
Salvation Jane
Cuisines: Breakfast & Brunch, Cafe
Average price: £26-45
Area: Liverpool Street / Broadgate
Address: 55 City Road
London EC1Y 1HQ
Phone: +44 20 7253 5273

#690
South London Pacific
Cuisines: Bar, Tapas
Average price: £11-25
Area: Oval, Kennington
Address: 340 Kennington Road
London SE11 4LD
Phone: +44 20 7820 9189

#691
The FRENCHIE
Cuisines: Street Vendor,
Food Stands, French
Area: Camden Town
Address: Camden Lock Market
London NW1 8AF

#692
Sushi Tetsu
Cuisines: Sushi Bar
Area: Clerkenwell
Address: 12 Jerusalem Passage
London EC1V 4JP
Phone: +44 20 3217 0090

#693
Chanteroy Cuisines:
Food, Deli **Average price:**
Under £10
Area: Wimbledon
Address: 233a Wimbledon Park Road
London SW18 5RJ
Phone: +44 20 8874 1446

#694
The Dairy
Cuisines: Bar, British
Average price: £11-25
Area: Clapham
Address: 16-17 The Pavement
London SW4 0HY
Phone: +44 20 7622 4165

#695
Cinnamon Coffee Shop
Cuisines: Cafe, Sandwiches,
Coffee & Tea
Average price: Under £10
Area: Wapping
Address: 103 Wapping Lane
London E1W 2RW
Phone: +44 29 7702 2323

#696
Banana Tree
Cuisines: Halal, Asian Fusion
Average price: £11-25
Area: Clapham Common,
Clapham Junction
Address: 75-79 Battersea Rise
London SW11 1HN
Phone: +44 20 7228 2828

#697
Vinoteca
Cuisines: Wine Bar, European
Average price: £11-25
Area: Marylebone
Address: 15 Seymour Place
London W1H 5BD
Phone: +44 20 7724 7288

#698
El Metro Restaurant
Cuisines: Spanish, Basque
Average price: £11-25
Area: Fulham, Fulham Broadway
Address: 10-12 Effie Road
London SW6 1TB
Phone: +44 20 7384 1264

#699
Il Convivio
Cuisines: Italian
Average price: Above £46
Area: Belgravia
Address: 143 Ebury Street
London SW1W 9QN
Phone: +44 20 7730 4099

#700
Bleecker St. Burger
Cuisines: Street Vendor, Burgers
Average price: Under £10
Area: Covent Garden, Strand
Address: Hartwell Street
London E8 3DU
Phone: +44 7712 540501

#701
Club Gascon
Cuisines: French
Average price: Above £46
Area: Farringdon
Address: 57 W Smithfield
London EC1A 9DS
Phone: +44 20 7600 6144

#702
Seven at Brixton
Cuisines: Spanish, Lounge, Cocktail Bar
Average price: £11-25
Address: 7 Market Row
London SW9 8LB

#703
The Rapscallion
Cuisines: Breakfast & Brunch, European,
Cocktail Bar
Average price: £11-25
Area: Clapham, Clapham Common
Address: 75 Venn Street
London SW4 0BD
Phone: +44 20 7787 6555

#704
Umu
Cuisines: Japanese
Average price: Above £46
Area: Mayfair
Address: 14-16 Bruton Place
London W1J 6LX
Phone: +44 20 7499 8881

#705
Rocca
Cuisines: Italian
Average price: £11-25
Area: South Kensington
Address: 73 Old Brompton Road
London SW7 3LD
Phone: +44 20 7225 3413

#706
Zilouf's
Cuisines: Asian Fusion, Bar,
Breakfast & Brunch
Average price: £11-25
Area: Islington
Address: 270 Upper Street
London N1 2UQ
Phone: +44 20 7226 1118

#707
The Cafe In The Crypt
Cuisines: Cafe
Average price: £11-25
Area: Covent Garden, Strand
Address: Trafalgar Square
London WC2N 4JJ
Phone: +44 20 7766 1100

#708
Lucky 7
Cuisines: American, Burgers,
Breakfast & Brunch
Average price: £11-25
Area: Notting Hill
Address: 127 Westbourne Park Rd
London W2 5QL
Phone: +44 20 7727 6771

#709
Strongroom Bar & Kitchen
Cuisines: Bar, British
Average price: £11-25
Area: Hoxton
Address: 120-124 Curtain Road
London EC2A 3SQ
Phone: +44 20 7426 5103

#710
Tas Pide
Cuisines: Turkish
Average price: £11-25
Area: South Bank, Southwark
Address: 20 - 22 New Globe Walk
London SE1 9DR
Phone: +44 20 7928 3300

#711
Le Pain Quotidien
Cuisines: Bakery, French, Belgian
Average price: £11-25
Area: Marylebone
Address: 72-75 Marylebone High Street
London W1U 5JW
Phone: +44 20 3657 6949

#712
Côte
Cuisines: Breakfast & Brunch, French
Average price: £11-25
Area: Soho
Address: 124-126 Wardour Street
London W1F 0TY
Phone: +44 20 7287 9280

#713
Wagamama
Cuisines: Japanese, Asian Fusion
Average price: £11-25
Area: Westminster
Address: Cardinal Place
London SW1E 5JE
Phone: +44 20 7828 0561

#714
Leon - The Strand
Cuisines: Mediterranean, Fast Food
Average price: Under £10
Area: Strand
Address: 73-76 The Strand
London WC2R 0DE
Phone: +44 20 7240 3070

#715
Dirty Burger
Cuisines: Burgers
Average price: Under £10
Area: Oval, South Lambeth
Address: 6 S Lambeth Road Vauxhall
London SW8 1SS
Phone: +44 20 7074 1444

#716
Antico Restaurant & Bar
Cuisines: Italian
Average price: £11-25
Area: Borough
Address: 214 Bermondsey Street
London SE1 3TQ
Phone: +44 20 7407 4682

#717
Carluccio's
Cuisines: Italian
Average price: £11-25
Area: Covent Garden
Address: Garrick Street
London WC2E 9BH
Phone: +44 20 7836 0990

#718
Tohbang
Cuisines: Korean
Average price: £11-25
Area: Bloomsbury
Address: 164 Clerkenwell Road
London EC1R 5DU
Phone: +44 20 7278 8674

#719
Kurz & Lang
Cuisines: Hot Dogs, German
Average price: Under £10
Area: Farringdon
Address: 1 Saint John Street
London EC1M 4AA
Phone: +44 20 7993 2923

#720
The Fellow
Cuisines: Lounge, Gastropub
Average price: £11-25
Area: King's Cross
Address: 24 York Way
London N1 9AA
Phone: +44 20 7837 3001

#721
Taro
Cuisines: Japanese, Sushi Bar
Average price: £11-25
Area: Bloomsbury
Address: 10 Old Compton Street
London W1D 4TF
Phone: +44 20 7439 2275

#722
Grand Bazaar
Cuisines: Turkish, Greek, Mediterranean
Average price: £11-25
Area: Marylebone
Address: 42 James Street
London W1U 1EX
Phone: +44 20 7224 1544

#723
Chipotle
Cuisines: Fast Food, Mexican
Average price: Under £10
Area: Angel, Islington
Address: 334 Upper Street
London N1 0PB
Phone: +44 20 7354 3686

#724
Royal Oak
Cuisines: Pub, British
Average price: £11-25
Area: Shoreditch, Bethnal Green
Address: 73 Columbia Road
London E2 7RG
Phone: +44 20 7729 2220

#725
The Thomas Cubitt
Cuisines: Gastropub
Average price: £26-45
Area: Belgravia
Address: 44 Elizabeth Street
London SW1W 9PA
Phone: +44 20 7730 6060

#726
The Gilbert Scott
Cuisines: Bar, British
Average price: Above £46
Area: King's Cross
Address: Euston Road
London NW1 2AR
Phone: +44 20 7278 3888

#727
Pizzeria Oregano
Cuisines: Italian
Average price: £11-25
Area: Angel, Islington
Address: 18-19 St Alban's Place
London N1 0NX
Phone: +44 20 7288 1123

#728
Ping Pong
Cuisines: Dim Sum
Average price: £11-25
Area: Marylebone
Address: 29 James Street
London W1U 1DZ
Phone: +44 20 7034 3100

#729
Sergio's Restaurant
Cuisines: Italian
Average price: Above £46
Area: Fitzrovia
Address: 84a Great Titchfield Street
London W1W 7QY
Phone: +44 20 7436 7301

#730
Salt Bar
Cuisines: British, Bar
Average price: £26-45
Area: Paddington
Address: 13 Edgware Road
London W2 2JE
Phone: +44 20 7402 1155

#731
Fairuz
Cuisines: Middle Eastern
Average price: £11-25
Area: Marylebone
Address: 3 Blandford Street
London W1U 3DA
Phone: +44 20 7486 8108

#732
Rasa Sayang
Cuisines: Malaysian, Chinese
Average price: Under £10
Area: Chinatown
Address: 5 Macclesfield Street
London W1D 6AY
Phone: +44 20 7734 1382

#733
Big Easy
Cuisines: American, Bar, Music Venues
Average price: £11-25
Area: Chelsea
Address: 332-334 Kings Road
London SW3 5UR
Phone: +44 20 7352 4071

#734
Leila's Shop
Cuisines: Grocery, Cafe
Average price: £11-25
Area: Shoreditch, Bethnal Green
Address: 17 Calvert Avenue
London E2 7JP
Phone: +44 20 7729 9789

#735
Fresco
Cuisines: Juice Bar, Middle Eastern
Average price: Under £10
Area: Bayswater
Address: 25 Westbourne Grove
London W2 4UA
Phone: +44 20 7221 2355

#736
Star Kebab House
Cuisines: Fast Food
Average price: Under £10
Area: Earls Court
Address: 178 Earls Court Road
London SW5 9QQ
Phone: +44 20 7370 4051

#737
FishWorks
Cuisines: Seafood
Average price: £26-45
Area: Marylebone
Address: 89 Marylebone High Street
London W1U 4QW
Phone: +44 20 7935 9796

#738
The Blue Legume
Cuisines: British, Breakfast & Brunch
Average price: £11-25
Area: Islington
Address: 177 Upper St
London N1 1RG
Phone: +44 20 7226 5858

#739
Ittenbari
Cuisines: Japanese
Average price: £11-25
Area: Piccadilly
Address: 84 Brewer Street
London W1F 9UB
Phone: +44 20 7287 1318

#740
Le Relais de Venise L'Entrecôte
Cuisines: French
Average price: £26-45
Area: The City
Address: 5 Throgmorton Street
London EC2N 2AD
Phone: +44 20 7638 6325

#741
The Clove Club
Cuisines: British, Cocktail Bar
Average price: Above £46
Area: Hoxton
Address: Shoreditch Town Hall
London EC1V 9LT
Phone: +44 20 7729 6496

#742
Violet Cakes
Cuisines: Desserts, Bakery, Cafe
Average price: £26-45
Area: Hackney Central
Address: 47 Wilton Way
London E8 3ED
Phone: +44 20 7275 8360

#743
The Yellow House
Cuisines: Pizza, European, Mediterranean
Average price: £11-25
Area: Bermondsey, Canada Water,
Rotherhithe, Surrey Quays
Address: 126 Lower Road
London SE16 2UE
Phone: +44 20 7231 8777

#744
Goddards at Greenwich
Cuisines: British
Average price: Under £10
Area: Greenwich
Address: 22 King William Walk
London SE10 9HU
Phone: +44 20 8305 9612

#745
M Moen & Sons
Cuisines: Meat Shop, Deli
Average price: £26-45
Area: Clapham
Address: 24 The Pavement
London SW4 0JA
Phone: +44 20 7622 1624

#746
El Rincon Latino
Cuisines: Spanish, Tapas Bar
Average price: £11-25
Area: Clapham
Address: 148 Clapham Manor St
London SW4 6BX
Phone: +44 20 7622 0599

#747
Al Waha
Cuisines: Middle Eastern
Average price: £26-45
Area: Bayswater
Address: 75 Westbourne Grove
London W2 4UL
Phone: +44 20 7229 0806

#748
The Crooked Well
Cuisines: Gastropub, British
Average price: £11-25
Area: Camberwell
Address: 16 Grove Lane
London SE5 8SY
Phone: +44 20 7252 7798

#749
Sasuke
Cuisines: Japanese
Average price: £11-25
Area: Soho
Address: 32 Great Windmill Street
London W1D 7LR
Phone: +44 20 7434 3362

#750
Opera Tavern
Cuisines: Tapas Bar
Average price: £26-45
Area: Covent Garden, Strand
Address: 23 Catherine Street
London WC2B 5JS
Phone: +44 20 7836 3680

#751
Hare & Tortoise
Cuisines: Chinese, Japanese
Average price: £11-25
Area: Bloomsbury
Address: 11-13 Brunswick Centre
London WC1N 1AF
Phone: +44 20 7278 9799

#752
Icebar
Cuisines: European, Lounge
Average price: £11-25
Area: Piccadilly
Address: 31-33 Heddon Street
London W1B 4BN
Phone: +44 20 7478 8910

#753
Leon - Carnaby Street
Cuisines: Deli, Mediterranean
Average price: £11-25
Area: Soho
Address: 35 Great Marlborough Street
London W1F 7JE
Phone: +44 20 7734 8057

#754
Burger & Lobster
Cuisines: American
Average price: £26-45
Area: The City
Address: 1 Bread Street
London EC4M 9SH

#755
The Kitchen @ Tower
Cuisines: Bakery, British,
Breakfast & Brunch
Average price: £11-25
Area: Aldgate, The City
Address: Byward Street
London EC3R 5BJ
Phone: +44 20 7481 3533

#756
Nando's
Cuisines: Portuguese, Chicken Wings
Average price: £11-25
Area: Noel Park, Wood Green
Address: Redvers Road
London N22 6EJ
Phone: +44 20 8889 2936

#757
YO! Sushi
Cuisines: Japanese
Average price: £26-45
Area: Paddington
Address: The Lawn Paddington Station
London W2 1HB
Phone: +44 20 7706 9550

#758
Stone Cave
Cuisines: Turkish
Average price: £11-25
Area: De Beauvoir, Kingsland
Address: 111 Kingsland High Street
London E8 2PB
Phone: +44 20 7241 4911

#759
Bar Story
Cuisines: Bar, British, Burgers
Average price: £11-25
Area: Peckham
Address: 213 Blenheim Grove
London SE15 4QL
Phone: +44 20 7635 6643

#760
Baozi Inn
Cuisines: Chinese
Average price: Under £10
Area: Chinatown
Address: 26 Newport Court
London WC2H 7JS
Phone: +44 20 7287 6877

#761
Hoxton Grill
Cuisines: Lounge, American
Average price: £11-25
Area: Liverpool Street / Broadgate
Address: 81 Great Eastern Street
London EC2A 3HU
Phone: +44 20 7739 9111

#762
City Càphê
Cuisines: Vietnamese
Average price: Under £10
Area: The City
Address: 17 Ironmonger Lane
London EC2V 8EY

#763
Portrait Restaurant
Cuisines: British, Tea Room
Average price: £26-45
Area: Trafalgar Square
Address: St Martin's Place
London WC2H 0HE
Phone: +44 20 7312 2490

#764
Electricity ShowRoom
Cuisines: Pub, Dance Club, British
Average price: £11-25
Area: Hoxton, Hoxton Square
Address: 39a Hoxton Square
London N1 6NN
Phone: +44 20 7739 3939

#765
EV Restaurant
Cuisines: Turkish
Average price: £11-25
Area: Southwark, Waterloo
Address: 97-99 Isabella Street
London SE1 8DD

#766
Barrica
Cuisines: Tapas Bar, Spanish
Average price: £26-45
Area: Fitzrovia
Address: 62 Goodge Street
London W1T 4NE
Phone: +44 20 7436 9448

#767
The Tommyfield
Cuisines: British
Average price: £11-25
Area: Kennington
Address: 185 Kennington Lane
London SE11 4EZ
Phone: +44 20 7735 1061

#768
Nando's
Cuisines: Portuguese
Average price: £11-25
Area: Soho
Address: 10 Frith Street
London W1D 3JF
Phone: +44 20 7494 0932

#769
Fish!
Cuisines: Fish & Chips, Seafood
Average price: £11-25
Area: London Bridge
Address: Cathedral Street
London SE1 9AL
Phone: +44 20 7407 3803

#770
Public House
Cuisines: British, Bar
Average price: £11-25
Area: Islington
Address: 54 Islington Park Street
London N1 1PX
Phone: +44 20 7359 6070

#771
Electric Diner
Cuisines: American
Average price: £11-25
Area: Notting Hill
Address: 191 Portobello Road
London W11 2ED
Phone: +44 20 7908 9696

#772
Pret A Manger
Cuisines: Sandwiches, Coffee & Tea
Average price: Under £10
Area: Bloomsbury
Address: 40 Bernard Street
London WC1N 1LE
Phone: +44 20 7932 5374

#773
Chilango Cuisines:
Mexican **Average price:**
Under £10
Area: Holborn
Address: 76 Chancery Lane
London WC2A 1AA
Phone: +44 20 7430 1231

#774
Thai Metro
Cuisines: Thai
Average price: £11-25
Area: Fitzrovia
Address: 38 Charlotte Street
London W1T 2NN
Phone: +44 20 7436 4201

#775
Joy King Lau
Cuisines: Dim Sum
Average price: £11-25
Area: Leicester Square
Address: 3 Leicester Street
London WC2H 7BL
Phone: +44 20 7437 1132

#776
Tamarind
Cuisines: Indian
Average price: £26-45
Area: Mayfair
Address: 20 Queen Street
London W1J 5PP
Phone: +44 20 7629 3561

#777
Fig & Olive
Cuisines: Mediterranean, European
Average price: £11-25
Area: Islington
Address: 151 Upper Street
London N1 1RA
Phone: +44 20 7354 2605

#778
Guanabara
Cuisines: Dance Club, Brazilian
Average price: £26-45
Area: Covent Garden
Address: Parker St & Drury Ln
London WC2B 5PW
Phone: +44 20 7242 8600

#779
The Narrow
Cuisines: Gastropub
Average price: £11-25
Area: Limehouse
Address: 44 Narrow Street
London E14 8DQ
Phone: +44 20 7592 7950

#780
Compton Arms
Cuisines: Pub, British
Average price: £26-45
Area: Islington
Address: 4 Compton Avenue
London N1 2XD
Phone: +44 20 7359 6883

#781
Sagar
Cuisines: Vegetarian, Vegan, Indian
Average price: £11-25
Area: Fitzrovia
Address: 17a Percy Street
London W1T 1DU
Phone: +44 20 7631 3319

#782
Manze's Eel Pie & Mash shop
Cuisines: Cafe, Fast Food
Area: Angel, Islington
Address: Chapel Market
London N1 0RW
Phone: +44 20 7278 8787

#783
Indian Zing
Cuisines: Indian
Average price: £11-25
Area: Hammersmith, Ravenscourt Park
Address: 236 King Street
London W6 0RF
Phone: +44 20 8748 2332

#784
Lamberts
Cuisines: British
Average price: Above £46
Area: Balham
Address: 2 Station Parade
London SW12 9AZ
Phone: +44 20 8675 2233

#785
10 Greek Street
Cuisines: European
Average price: £26-45
Area: Bloomsbury
Address: 10 Greek Street
London W1D 4DH
Phone: +44 20 7734 4677

#786
Little Italy
Cuisines: Italian, Lounge
Average price: £26-45
Area: Bloomsbury
Address: 21 Frith Street
London W1D 4RN
Phone: +44 20 7734 4737

#787
Hummus Bros
Cuisines: Mediterranean, Greek
Average price: Under £10
Area: Bloomsbury
Address: 37-63 Southampton Row
London WC1B 4DA
Phone: +44 20 7404 7079

#788
My Old Dutch Pancake House
Cuisines: Creperie, Desserts
Average price: £11-25
Area: Bloomsbury
Address: 131-132 High Holborn
London WC1V 6PS
Phone: +44 20 7242 5200

#789
Okan
Cuisines: Japanese, Street Vendor
Average price: Under £10
Area: Coldharbour Lane/ Herne Hill
Address: Unit 39
London SW9 8PS

#790
Birley's Salt Beef Bar
Cuisines: Sandwiches
Average price: Under £10
Area: Canary Wharf, Isle of Dogs
Address: 1 Canada Square
London E14 5AX
Phone: +44 20 7719 1163

#791
Assaggi
Cuisines: Italian
Average price: £26-45
Area: Notting Hill
Address: 39 Chepstow Place
London W2 4TS
Phone: +44 20 7792 5501

#792
Firefly Bar & Thai Kitchen
Cuisines: Bar, Thai
Average price: £11-25
Area: Balham
Address: 3 Station Parade
London SW12 9AZ
Phone: +44 20 8673 9796

#793
Apsleys
Cuisines: Italian, Mediterranean
Average price: Above £46
Area: Hyde Park
Address: The Lanesborough Hotel
London SW1X 7TA
Phone: +44 20 7259 5599

#794
Kingly Court
Cuisines: Cafe, Shopping Center
Area: Soho
Address: Kingly Court
London W1F 9PY

#795
Angelus Restaurant
Cuisines: French
Average price: Above £46
Area: Paddington
Address: 4 Bathurst Street
London W2 2SD
Phone: +44 20 7402 0083

#796
Trattoria Montebianco
Cuisines: Italian
Average price: £11-25
Area: Fitzrovia
Address: 86 Cleveland Street
London W1T 6NQ
Phone: +44 20 7387 2375

#797
Le Peche Mignon
Cuisines: Coffee & Tea, French
Average price: Under £10
Area: Lower Holloway
Address: 6 Ronalds Road
London N5 1XH
Phone: +44 20 7607 1826

#798
Anfa Café
Cuisines: Coffee & Tea, Sandwiches
Average price: Under £10
Area: Farringdon
Address: 102 St John Street
London EC1M 4EH
Phone: +44 20 7490 7662

#799
Baltic Bar and Restaurant
Cuisines: European, Polish
Average price: £26-45
Area: Southwark
Address: 74 Blackfriars Road
London SE1 8AH
Phone: +44 20 7928 1111

#800
Malaysia Hall Canteen
Cuisines: Ethnic Food, Malaysian
Average price: Under £10
Area: Bayswater
Address: 30-34 Queensborough Terrace
London W2 3ST
Phone: +44 871 961 8354

#801
Cheyne Walk Brasserie
Cuisines: French, Bar
Average price: Above £46
Area: Chelsea
Address: 50 Cheyne Walk
London SW3 5LR
Phone: +44 20 7376 8787

#802
Fish Central
Cuisines: Seafood
Average price: £11-25
Area: Barbican
Address: 143-145 Central Street
London EC1V 8AP
Phone: +44 20 7253 0229

#803
Pizza Express
Cuisines: Pizza, Italian
Average price: £11-25
Area: Greenwich
Address: 4 Greenwich Church Street
London SE10 9BG
Phone: +44 20 8853 2770

#804
The Palmerston
Cuisines: Gastropub
Average price: £26-45
Area: East Dulwich
Address: 91 Lordship Lane
London SE22 8EP
Phone: +44 20 8693 1629

#805
Cocomaya
Cuisines: Bakery, Breakfast & Brunch
Average price: £11-25
Area: Paddington
Address: 12 Connaught Street
London W2 2AF
Phone: +44 20 7706 2883

#806
Le Boudin Blanc
Cuisines: French
Average price: £26-45
Area: Mayfair
Address: 5 Trebeck Street
London W1J 7LT
Phone: +44 20 7499 3292

#807
Polpo
Cuisines: Italian
Average price: £11-25
Area: Covent Garden, Strand
Address: 6 Maiden Lane
London WC2E 7NA
Phone: +44 20 7836 8448

#808
The Canton Arms
Cuisines: Gastropub
Average price: £11-25
Area: Oval, South Lambeth
Address: 177 S Lambeth Road
London SW8 1XP
Phone: +44 20 7582 8710

#809
Princess Victoria
Cuisines: Gastropub, Venues,
Event Space, Pub
Average price: Above £46
Area: Acton
Address: 217 Uxbridge Road
London W12 9DH
Phone: +44 20 8749 5886

#810
Don Quixote
Cuisines: Sandwiches, Deli
Average price: Under £10
Area: Covent Garden
Address: 101 Kingsway
London WC2B 6QU
Phone: +44 20 7430 2413

#811
Gallipoli Bazaar
Cuisines: Turkish, Moroccan
Average price: £11-25
Area: Angel, Islington
Address: 107 Upper Street
London N1 1QN
Phone: +44 20 7226 5333

#812
Bar Kick
Cuisines: Sports Bar, Burgers,
Mediterranean
Average price: £11-25
Area: Hoxton
Address: 127 Shoreditch High Street
London E1 6JE
Phone: +44 20 7739 8700

#813
Bento Cafe
Cuisines: Japanese
Average price: £11-25
Area: Camden Town
Address: 9 Parkway
London NW1 7PG
Phone: +44 20 7482 3990

#814
Daylesford Organic
Cuisines: British, Specialty Food
Average price: £26-45
Area: Notting Hill
Address: 208-212 Westbourne Grove
London W11 2RH
Phone: +44 20 7313 8050

#815
Kipferl Austrian Coffeehouse
Cuisines: Coffee & Tea,
European, Austrian
Average price: £11-25
Area: Angel, Islington
Address: 20 Camden Passage
London N1 8ED
Phone: +44 20 7704 1555

#816
Dans Le Noir
Cuisines: French
Average price: Above £46
Area: Clerkenwell
Address: 30-31 Clerkenwell Green
London EC1R 0DU
Phone: +44 20 7253 1100

#817
Kulu Kulu Sushi
Cuisines: Japanese
Average price: £11-25
Area: Soho
Address: 76 Brewer Street
London W1F 9TX
Phone: +44 20 7734 7316

#818
Elliot's
Cuisines: Cafe, British
Average price: £26-45
Area: London Bridge
Address: 12 Stoney Street
London SE1 9AD
Phone: +44 20 7403 7436

#819
Pizzeria Rustica
Cuisines: Pizza, Italian
Average price: £11-25
Area: Richmond Upon Thames
Address: 32 The Quadrant
Richmond TW9 1DN
Phone: +44 20 8332 6262

#820
Benugo @ BFI
Cuisines: Bar, British
Average price: £11-25
Area: Southwark
Address: 2166 Belvedere Rd
London SE1 8XT
Phone: +44 20 7928 3232

#821
Original Maids Of Honour
Cuisines: British, Coffee & Tea
Average price: £11-25
Area: Kew
Address: 288-290 Kew Road
Richmond TW9 3DU
Phone: +44 20 8940 2752

#822
Wagamama
Cuisines: Japanese, Asian Fusion
Average price: £11-25
Area: Soho
Address: 10a Lexington Street
London W1F 0LD
Phone: +44 20 7292 0990

#823
Smiths Of Smithfield
Cuisines: British
Average price: £26-45
Area: Farringdon
Address: 67-77a Charterhouse Street
London EC1M 6HJ
Phone: +44 20 7251 7950

#824
Leon - Spitelfields
Cuisines: Fast Food, Mediterranean
Average price: Under £10
Area: Spitalfields
Address: 3 Crispin Place
London E1 6DW
Phone: +44 20 7247 4369

#825
The Princess of Shoreditch
Cuisines: British, Gastropub
Average price: £26-45
Area: Liverpool Street / Broadgate
Address: 76-78 Paul Street
London EC2A 4NE
Phone: +44 20 7729 9270

#826
Imperial China
Cuisines: Chinese
Average price: £11-25
Area: Chinatown
Address: 25a Lisle Street
London WC2H 7BA
Phone: +44 20 7734 3388

#827
The Owl & Pussycat
Cuisines: Pub, British
Average price: £11-25
Area: Shoreditch, Bethnal Green
Address: 34 Redchurch Street
London E2 7DP
Phone: +44 20 7613 3628

#828
Eat Tokyo
Cuisines: Sushi Bar, Japanese
Average price: £11-25
Area: Trafalgar Square
Address: 15 Whitcomb Street
London WC2H 7HA
Phone: +44 20 7930 6117

#829
Mari Vanna
Cuisines: Russian, Breakfast & Brunch
Average price: £26-45
Area: Hyde Park
Address: 116 Knightsbridge
London SW1X 7PJ
Phone: +44 20 7225 3122

#830
Chennai Dosa
Cuisines: Vegetarian, Indian
Average price: Under £10
Area: Stonebridge Park
Address: 529 High Road
Wembley HA0 2DH
Phone: +44 20 8782 8822

#831
EAT.
Cuisines: Breakfast & Brunch,
Sandwiches, British
Average price: Under £10
Area: Marylebone
Address: 319 Regent Street
London W1B 2HU
Phone: +44 20 7636 8309

#832
Vivat Bacchus
Cuisines: European, Wine Bar
Average price: £26-45
Area: Farringdon
Address: 47 Farringdon Street
London EC4A 4LL
Phone: +44 20 7353 2648

#833
Camino
Cuisines: Bar, Spanish, Basque
Average price: £11-25
Area: King's Cross
Address: 3 Varnishers Yard
London N1 9AF
Phone: +44 20 7841 7331

#834
Royal China
Cuisines: Chinese
Average price: £26-45
Area: Canary Wharf, Isle of Dogs
Address: 30 Westferry Circus
London E14 8RR
Phone: +44 20 7719 0888

#835
Four Seasons
Cuisines: Chinese
Average price: £11-25
Area: Chinatown
Address: 12 Gerrard Street
London W1D 5PR
Phone: +44 20 7494 0870

#836
Salumeria Dino
Cuisines: Cafe, Deli
Average price: Under £10
Area: Fitzrovia
Address: 15 Charlotte Place
London W1B 1AP
Phone: +44 20 7580 3938

#837
Old Fountain
Cuisines: Pub, Gastropub
Average price: £11-25
Area: Barbican
Address: 3 Baldwin Street
London EC1V 9NU
Phone: +44 20 7253 2970

#838
Buenos Aires Café
Cuisines: Argentine
Average price: £26-45
Area: Blackheath
Address: 17 Royal Parade
London SE3 0TL
Phone: +44 20 8318 5333

#839
Chicks on Fire
Cuisines: Chicken Wings,
Barbeque, Diner
Average price: Under £10
Area: Holloway
Address: 11 Hercules Street
London N7 6AT
Phone: +44 20 3659 7491

#840
**The Dining Room
at The Goring Hotel**
Cuisines: British
Average price: Above £46
Area: Belgravia
Address: 15 Beeston Place
London SW1W 0JW
Phone: +44 20 7396 9000

#841
Sufi Restaurant
Cuisines: Persian/Iranian
Average price: £11-25
Area: Acton
Address: 70 Askew Road
London W12 9BJ
Phone: +44 20 8834 4888

#842
Ffiona's Restaurant
Cuisines: British
Average price: £11-25
Area: Kensington
Address: 51 Kensington Church Street
London W8 4BA
Phone: +44 20 7937 4152

#843
Battersea Barge
Cuisines: Restaurant
Average price: £11-25
Area: Nine Elms, South Lambeth
Address: Nine Elms Lane
London SW8 5DA
Phone: +44 20 7498 0004

#844
Jai Krishna
Cuisines: Indian, Vegetarian, Pakistani
Average price: Under £10
Area: Stroud Green
Address: 161 Stroud Green Road
London N4 3PZ
Phone: +44 20 7272 1680

#845
The Roebuck
Cuisines: Pub, British
Average price: £11-25
Area: Borough
Address: 50 Great Dover Street
London SE1 4YG
Phone: +44 20 7357 7324

#846
Pixxa Pizza al taglio
Cuisines: Pizza, Italian
Average price: Under £10
Area: Farringdon
Address: 8 St John Street
London EC1M 4AY
Phone: +44 7554 990171

#847
Bread Street Kitchen
Cuisines: Bar, British
Average price: £26-45
Area: The City
Address: 10 Bread Street
London EC4M 9AF
Phone: +44 20 7592 1616

#848
Giant Robot
Cuisines: Italian, American
Average price: £11-25
Area: Clerkenwell, Farringdon
Address: 45 Clerkenwell Road
London EC1M 5RS
Phone: +44 20 7065 6810

#849
Cafe Sol
Cuisines: Bar, Mexican
Average price: £11-25
Area: Clapham, Clapham Common
Address: 56 Clapham High Street
London SW4 7UL
Phone: +44 20 7498 8558

#850
A Little Of What You Fancy
Cuisines: Coffee & Tea, British
Average price: £11-25
Area: Dalston
Address: 464 Kingsland Rd
London E8 4AE
Phone: +44 20 7275 0060

#851
The Easton
Cuisines: Pub, Gastropub
Average price: £11-25
Area: Clerkenwell
Address: 22 Easton Street
London WC1X 0DS
Phone: +44 20 7278 7608

#852
Tatra
Cuisines: Polish
Average price: £11-25
Area: Shepherd's Bush
Address: 24 Goldhawk Road
London W12 8DH
Phone: +44 20 8749 8193

#853
The Fish & Chip Shop
Cuisines: Fish & Chips, British
Average price: £11-25
Area: Islington
Address: 189 Upper Street
London N1 1RQ
Phone: +44 20 3227 0979

#854
Brindisa Spanish Foods
Cuisines: Deli, Delicatessen
Average price: £26-45
Area: London Bridge
Address: The Floral Hall Stoney Street
London SE1 9AF
Phone: +44 20 7407 1036

#855
Megan's
Cuisines: Deli, British,
Breakfast & Brunch
Average price: £11-25
Area: West Brompton
Address: 571 Kings Road
London SW6 2EB
Phone: +44 20 7371 7837

#856
Premises Cafe/Bistro
Cuisines: Breakfast & Brunch,
Cafe, Bistro
Average price: Under £10
Area: Shoreditch, Haggerston
Address: 209 Hackney Road
London E2 8JL
Phone: +44 20 7684 2230

#857
Duck Egg Café
Cuisines: Cafe
Average price: £11-25
Area: Coldharbour Lane/ Herne Hill
Address: 424 Coldharbour Lane
London SW9 8LF
Phone: +44 20 7274 8972

#858
B Bar
Cuisines: British, Bar
Average price: £11-25
Area: Westminster
Address: 43 Buckingham Palace Road
London SW1W 0PP
Phone: +44 20 7958 7000

#859
Manna
Cuisines: Vegetarian, Vegan,
Gluten-Free
Average price: £26-45
Area: Chalk Farm, Primrose Hill
Address: 4 Erskine Road
London NW3 3AJ
Phone: +44 20 7722 8028

#860
Roxy Bar & Screen
Cuisines: Bar, Cinema, British
Average price: £26-45
Area: Borough
Address: 128-132 Borough High Street
London SE1 1LB
Phone: +44 20 7407 4057

#861
The Dining Plaice
Cuisines: Fish & Chips
Average price: £11-25
Area: Soho
Address: 20 Berwick Street
London W1F 0PY
Phone: +44 20 7437 3280

#862
Meson Don Felipe
Cuisines: Wine Bar, Spanish, Basque
Average price: £11-25
Area: Southwark, Waterloo
Address: 53 The Cut
London SE1 8LF
Phone: +44 20 7928 3237

#863
Pizza East
Cuisines: Pizza, Italian
Average price: £11-25
Area: Kensal Town
Address: 310 Portobello Road
London W10 5TA
Phone: +44 20 8969 4500

#864
Albion
Cuisines: British, Bakery, Patisserie/Cake
Shop
Average price: £11-25
Area: Shoreditch
Address: 2-4 Boundary Street
London E2 7DD
Phone: +44 20 7729 1051

#865
Polpo
Cuisines: Italian, Bar
Average price: £11-25
Area: Soho
Address: 41 Beak Street
London W1F 9SB
Phone: +44 20 7734 4479

#866
Mint Leaf
Cuisines: Indian, Pakistani, Bar
Average price: £26-45
Area: St James's, Trafalgar Square
Address: 4 Suffolk Place
London SW1Y 4HX
Phone: +44 20 7930 9020

#867
Jamies Italian
Cuisines: Italian
Average price: £11-25
Area: Kingston Upon Thames
Address: 19-23 High St
Kingston KT1 1LL
Phone: +44 20 3326 4300

#868
Searcy's St Pancras Grand Restaurant and Champagne Bar
Cuisines: Champagne Bar, British
Average price: £26-45
Area: King's Cross
Address: Euston Road
London N1C 4QL
Phone: +44 20 7870 9900

#869
Wagamama
Cuisines: Japanese, Asian Fusion
Average price: £11-25
Area: Bloomsbury
Address: 4A Streatham Street
London WC1A 1JB
Phone: +44 20 7323 9223

#870
Lupita
Cuisines: Mexican
Average price: £11-25
Area: Strand
Address: 13-15 Villiers Street
London WC2N 6ND
Phone: +44 20 7930 5355

#871
Tayyabs
Cuisines: Indian, Pakistani
Average price: £11-25
Area: Whitechapel
Address: 83-89 Fieldgate Street
London E1 1JU
Phone: +44 20 7247 9543

#872
Chi Noodle Bar and Restaurant
Cuisines: Asian Fusion
Average price: £11-25
Area: Blackfriars, Holborn
Address: 5 New Bridge St
London EC4V 6AB
Phone: +44 20 7353 2409

#873
Matsuri St. James's
Cuisines: Japanese, Sushi Bar
Average price: Above £46
Area: St James's
Address: 15 Bury Street
London SW1Y 6AL
Phone: +44 20 7839 1101

#874
Behesht
Cuisines: Persian/Iranian
Average price: £11-25
Area: Kensal Green, Kensal Rise
Address: 1082-1084 Harrow Road
London NW10 5NL
Phone: +44 20 8964 4477

#875
Two Point **Cuisines:**
Thai **Average price:**
£11-25
Area: Marylebone
Address: 26 Crawford Street
London W1H 1LL
Phone: +44 20 7724 9079

#876
Jerk City
Cuisines: Caribbean, British
Average price: £11-25
Area: Soho
Address: 189 Wardour Street
London W1F 8ZD
Phone: +44 20 7287 2878

#877
SUSHISAMBA London
Cuisines: Asian Fusion, Sushi Bar
Average price: Above £46
Area: Aldgate
Address: 110 BiShopgate
London EC2N 4AY
Phone: +44 20 3640 7330

#878
Tortilla
Cuisines: Mexican, Fast Food
Average price: Under £10
Area: Angel, Islington
Address: 13 Islington High Street
London N1 9LQ
Phone: +44 20 7833 3103

#879
The Rose Lounge
Cuisines: Tea Room, British
Average price: £26-45
Area: St James's
Address: 6 Waterloo Place
London SW1Y 4AN
Phone: +44 20 7747 2200

#880
Tap Coffee
Cuisines: Coffee & Tea, Cafe
Average price: Under £10
Area: Soho
Address: 193 Wardour Street
London W1F 8ZF
Phone: +44 20 7580 2163

#881
St. James's Hotel and Club
Cuisines: Hotel, British
Average price: Above £46
Area: Piccadilly
Address: 7-8 Park Place
London SW1A 1LS
Phone: +44 20 7316 1600

#882
The Quarters Cafe
Cuisines: Coffee & Tea, Asian Fusion
Average price: Under £10
Area: Highgate
Address: 267 Archway Road
London N6 5BS
Phone: +44 7955 383233

#883
Bellevue Rendezvous
Cuisines: French
Average price: £11-25
Area: Balham, Wandsworth Common
Address: 218 Trinity Road
London SW17 7HP
Phone: +44 20 8767 5810

#884
The Food Joint
Cuisines: Barbeque, Fast Food
Average price: Under £10
Area: Coldharbour Lane/ Herne Hill
Address: Unit 87
London SW9 8PS

#885
Roadhouse Restaurant
Cuisines: Bar, British
Average price: £11-25
Area: Covent Garden, Strand
Address: Jubilee Hall 35
London WC2E 8BE
Phone: +44 20 7240 6001

#886
Zizzi
Cuisines: Italian
Average price: £11-25
Area: Westminster
Address: 15 Cardinal Walk
London SW1E 5JE
Phone: +44 20 7821 0402

#887
Yaki
Cuisines: Japanese, Asian Fusion, Cafe
Average price: Under £10
Area: Fitzrovia
Address: 53 Goodge Street
London W1T 1TG
Phone: +44 20 7636 9887

#888
The Garden Gate
Cuisines: Pub, British
Average price: £11-25
Area: Hampstead Heath
Address: 14 S End Road
London NW3 2QE
Phone: +44 20 7435 4938

#889
Camellia's Tea House
Cuisines: Coffee & Tea, Tea Room
Average price: £11-25
Area: Soho
Address: 2 12 Kingly Court
London W1B 5PW
Phone: +44 20 7734 9939

#890
Pret A Manger
Cuisines: Sandwiches, Coffee & Tea
Average price: Under £10
Area: King's Cross
Address: 296 Pentonville Road
London N1 9NR
Phone: +44 20 7932 5369

#891
The Somers Town Coffee House
Cuisines: British, Pub
Average price: £11-25
Area: Euston
Address: 60 Chalton Street
London NW1 1HS
Phone: +44 20 7387 7377

#892
Strada
Cuisines: Italian
Average price: £11-25
Area: Fitzrovia
Address: 9-10 Market Place
London W1W 8AQ
Phone: +44 20 7580 4644

#893
The Jones Family Project
Cuisines: Breakfast & Brunch,
British, Cafe
Average price: £11-25
Area: Liverpool Street / Broadgate
Address: 78 Great Eastern Street
London EC2A 3JL
Phone: +44 20 7739 1740

#894
Banana Tree
Cuisines: Halal, Asian Fusion
Average price: £11-25
Area: West Hampstead
Address: 237-239 W End Lane
London NW6 1XN
Phone: +44 20 7431 7808

#895
Souk Bazaar
Cuisines: Moroccan
Average price: £11-25
Area: Covent Garden
Address: 27 Litchfield Street
London WC2H 9NJ
Phone: +44 20 7240 1796

#896
The Cut Bar
Cuisines: Bar, Coffee & Tea,
Breakfast & Brunch
Average price: £11-25
Area: Southwark, Waterloo
Address: 66 The Cut
London SE1 8LZ
Phone: +44 20 7928 4400

#897
Karpo
Cuisines: European
Average price: £11-25
Area: Bloomsbury
Address: 23 Euston Road
London NW1 2SB
Phone: +44 20 7843 2221

#898
Couscous Darna
Cuisines: Moroccan
Average price: £11-25
Area: South Kensington
Address: 91 Old Brompton Road
London SW7 3LD
Phone: +44 20 7584 2919

#899
Mama Thai
Cuisines: Thai
Average price: Under £10
Area: Aldgate
Address: 10 Toynbee Street
London E1 7NE

#900
Satay Cocktail Bar & Restaurant
Cuisines: Indonesian
Average price: £11-25
Area: Brixton
Address: 447 Coldharbour Lane
London SW9 8LP
Phone: +44 844 474 6080

#901
Eyre Brothers
Cuisines: Portuguese
Average price: £26-45
Area: Liverpool Street / Broadgate
Address: 70 Leonard Street
London EC2A 4QX
Phone: +44 20 7613 5346

#902
Eight Over Eight
Cuisines: Asian Fusion
Average price: £26-45
Area: Chelsea
Address: 392 Kings Road
London SW3 5UZ
Phone: +44 20 7349 9934

#903
Tortilla
Cuisines: Mexican, Fast Food
Average price: Under £10
Area: Southwark
Address: 106 Southwark Street
London SE1 0TA
Phone: +44 20 7620 0285

#904
Bermondsey Street Coffee
Cuisines: Coffee & Tea, Sandwiches
Average price: £11-25
Area: Borough
Address: 163-167 Bermondsey Street
London SE1 3UW
Phone: +44 20 7403 7655

#905
La Chapelle
Cuisines: French
Average price: £26-45
Area: Spitalfields
Address: 35 Spital Square
London E1 6DY
Phone: +44 20 7299 0400

#906
The White Hart
Cuisines: Pub, British
Average price: £11-25
Area: Southwark, Waterloo
Address: 29 Cornwall Road
London SE1 8TJ
Phone: +44 20 7928 9190

#907
Moka
Cuisines: Coffee & Tea, Cafe
Average price: £11-25
Area: Harringay, Hornsey Vale
Address: 5 Wightman Road
London N4 1RQ
Phone: +44 20 8340 8664

#908
Zengi
Cuisines: Turkish, Lebanese
Average price: £11-25
Area: Brick Lane, Shoreditch
Address: 44 Commercial Street
London E1 6LT
Phone: +44 20 7426 0700

#909
Orjowan Lebanese Cuisine
Cuisines: Middle Eastern
Average price: £11-25
Area: South Kensington
Address: 6 Kenway Road
London SW5 0RR
Phone: +44 20 7370 3074

#910
Pret A Manger
Cuisines: Coffee & Tea, Sandwiches
Average price: £11-25
Area: Aldgate
Address: 192 BiShopgate
London EC2M 4NR
Phone: +44 20 7932 5272

#911
Geronimo Inns
Cuisines: Pub, Gastropub
Average price: £11-25
Area: Wandsworth
Address: 21 Alma Road
London SW18 1AA
Phone: +44 20 8877 8820

#912
Restaurant Story
Cuisines: European
Average price: Above £46
Area: London Bridge
Address: 201 Tooley Street
London SE1 2UE
Phone: +44 20 7183 2117

#913
Brixton Cornercopia
Cuisines: Cafe, Grocery
Average price: Under £10
Area: Coldharbour Lane/ Herne Hill
Address: 65 Brixton Village Market
London SW9 8PS
Phone: +44 7919 542233

#914
Masala Zone
Cuisines: Indian, Vegetarian, Halal
Average price: £11-25
Area: Covent Garden
Address: 48 Floral Street
London WC2E 9DA
Phone: +44 20 7379 0101

#915
The Only Running Footman
Cuisines: British, Gastropub
Average price: £11-25
Area: Mayfair
Address: 5 Charles Street
London W1J 5DF
Phone: +44 20 7499 2988

#916
Nemnem
Cuisines: Vietnamese
Average price: Under £10
Area: Bloomsbury
Address: 144 Clerkenwell Road
London EC1R 5DP
Phone: +44 20 7278 4123

#917
L'Eto Caffe
Cuisines: Cafe
Average price: £11-25
Area: Soho
Address: 155 Wardour Street
London W1F 8WG
Phone: +44 20 7494 4991

#918
Hush
Cuisines: European
Average price: £26-45
Area: Marylebone
Address: 8 Lancashire Court
London W1S 1EY
Phone: +44 20 7659 1500

#919
El Pirata
Cuisines: Spanish
Average price: £26-45
Area: Mayfair
Address: 5-6 Down Street
London W1J 7AQ
Phone: +44 20 7491 3810

#920
Yalla Yalla
Cuisines: Middle Eastern
Average price: £11-25
Area: Fitzrovia
Address: 12 Winsley Street
London W1W 8HQ
Phone: +44 20 7637 4748

#921
Draft House Tower Bridge
Cuisines: Gastropub, Pub
Average price: £11-25
Area: London Bridge, Shad Thames
Address: 206-208 Tower Bridge Road
London SE1 2UP
Phone: +44 20 7378 9995

#922
La Perla Bar & Grill
Cuisines: Mexican, Tex-Mex, Bar
Average price: £11-25
Area: Covent Garden, Strand
Address: 28 Maiden Lane
London WC2E 7JS
Phone: +44 20 7240 7400

#923
Masala Zone
Cuisines: Indian, Vegetarian, Halal
Average price: £11-25
Area: South Kensington
Address: 147 Earls Court Road
London SW5 9RQ
Phone: +44 20 7373 0220

#924
Champor-Champor
Cuisines: Malaysian, Thai
Average price: £26-45
Area: Borough
Address: 62-64 Weston Street
London SE1 3QJ
Phone: +44 20 7403 4600

#925
Langan's Brasserie
Cuisines: French, British
Average price: £26-45
Area: Mayfair
Address: Stratton Street
London W1J 8LB
Phone: +44 20 7491 8822

#926
Wagamama
Cuisines: Japanese, Asian Fusion
Average price: £11-25
Area: Kensington
Address: 26 Kensington High Street
London W8 4PF
Phone: +44 20 7376 1717

#927
City Best Kebab Takeaway
Cuisines: Fast Food
Average price: Under £10
Area: Hoxton, Hoxton Square
Address: 10 Pitfield Street
London N1 6HA
Phone: +44 20 7729 7632

#928
101 Thai Kitchen
Cuisines: Thai
Average price: £11-25
Area: Hammersmith, Ravenscourt Park
Address: 352 King Street
London W6 0RX
Phone: +44 20 8746 6888

#929
Novikov
Cuisines: Asian Fusion, Italian, Lounge
Average price: Above £46
Area: Mayfair
Address: 50 Berkeley Street
London W1J 8HA
Phone: +44 20 7399 4330

#930
Koya Bar
Cuisines: Japanese
Average price: £26-45
Area: Soho
Address: 50 Frith Street
London W1D 4SQ

#931
Kolossi Grill
Cuisines: Greek, Mediterranean
Average price: £11-25
Area: Clerkenwell
Address: 56-60 Rosebery Avenue
London EC1R 4RR
Phone: +44 20 7278 5758

#932
Galicia Restaurant
Cuisines: Spanish
Average price: £11-25
Area: Kensal Town
Address: 323 Portobello Road
London W10 5SY
Phone: +44 20 8969 3539

#933
Green Valley
Cuisines: Grocery, Deli
Average price: £11-25
Area: Marylebone
Address: 36-37 Upper Berkeley Street
London W1H 5QF
Phone: +44 20 7402 7385

#934
Bloomsbury Coffee House
Cuisines: Coffee & Tea, Cafe
Average price: Under £10
Area: Bloomsbury
Address: 20 Tavistock Place
London WC1H 9RE

#935
Chaat
Cuisines: Indian
Average price: £11-25
Area: Shoreditch, Bethnal Green
Address: 36 Redchurch Street
London E2 7DP
Phone: +44 20 7739 9595

#936
Green Cottage
Cuisines: Chinese
Average price: £11-25
Area: Swiss Cottage
Address: 9 New College Parade
London NW3 5EP
Phone: +44 20 7722 7892

#937
Rivington Bar & Grill
Cuisines: British
Average price: £26-45
Area: Greenwich
Address: 178 Greenwich High Road
London SE10 8NN
Phone: +44 20 8293 9270

#938
The Jugged Hare
Cuisines: Brasserie, British, European
Average price: £26-45
Area: Barbican
Address: 49 Chiswell Street
London EC1Y 4SA
Phone: +44 20 7614 0134

#939
Benihana
Cuisines: Japanese, Sushi Bar,
Steakhouse
Average price: £26-45
Area: Chelsea
Address: 77 Kings Road
London SW3 4NX
Phone: +44 20 7376 7799

#940
Kêu!
Cuisines: Vietnamese
Average price: Under £10
Area: Hoxton
Address: 332 Old Street
London EC1V 9DR
Phone: +44 20 7739 1164

#941
Satay House
Cuisines: Malaysian, Halal
Average price: £11-25
Area: Paddington
Address: 13 Sale Place
London W2 1PX
Phone: +44 20 7723 6763

#942
Rodizio Rico
Cuisines: Brazilian
Average price: £11-25
Area: Angel, Islington
Address: 77 Upper Street
London N1 0NU
Phone: +44 20 7354 1076

#943
Red Dog Saloon
Cuisines: American
Average price: £11-25
Area: Hoxton, Hoxton Square
Address: 37 Hoxton Square
London N1 6NN
Phone: +44 20 3551 8014

#944
Five Guys
Cuisines: Burgers, Hot Dogs
Average price: £11-25
Area: Covent Garden
Address: 1-3 Long Acre
London WC2E 9LH
Phone: +44 20 7240 2057

#945
Tapas Brindisa
Cuisines: Spanish, Tapas Bar, Basque
Average price: £26-45
Area: Soho
Address: 46 Broadwick Street
London W1F 7AF
Phone: +44 20 7534 1690

#946
Gold Mine
Cuisines: Chinese
Average price: £11-25
Area: Bayswater
Address: 102 Queensway
London W2 3RR
Phone: +44 20 7792 8331

#947
Christopher's
Cuisines: American, Bar, British
Average price: £11-25
Area: Covent Garden, Strand
Address: 18 Wellington Street
London WC2E 7DD
Phone: +44 20 7240 4222

#948
The Old Queen's Head
Cuisines: Bar, Music Venues, British
Average price: £11-25
Area: Angel, Islington
Address: 44 Essex Road
London N1 8LN
Phone: +44 20 7354 9993

#949
Côte
Cuisines: French
Average price: £11-25
Area: Covent Garden, Strand
Address: 17-21 Tavistock Street
London WC2E 7PA
Phone: +44 20 7379 9991

#950
Nando's
Cuisines: Portuguese
Average price: Under £10
Area: Camden Town, Chalk Farm
Address: 57-58 Chalk Farm Road
London NW1 8AN
Phone: +44 20 7424 9040

#951
The Savoy Grill
Cuisines: French, British
Average price: Above £46
Area: Strand **Address:**
100 Strand London WC2R
0EU **Phone:** +44 20 7592
1600

#952
Pizarro
Cuisines: Spanish
Average price: £26-45
Area: Borough
Address: 194 Bermondsey Street
London SE1 3TQ
Phone: +44 20 7407 7339

#953
Cafe Helen
Cuisines: Cafe
Average price: Under £10
Area: Paddington
Address: 105 Edgware Road
London W2 2HX
Phone: +44 20 7402 2072

#954
Chipotle
Cuisines: Mexican
Average price: Under £10
Area: Bloomsbury
Address: 114-116 Charing Cross Road
London WC2H 0JR
Phone: +44 20 7836 8491

#955
Italia Uno
Cuisines: Fast Food, Coffee & Tea
Average price: Under £10
Area: Fitzrovia
Address: 91 Charlotte Street
London W1T 4PX
Phone: +44 20 7637 5326

#956
Chris's Fish Bar
Cuisines: Fish & Chips
Average price: £26-45
Area: Chiswick
Address: 19 Turnham Green Terr
London W4 1RG
Phone: +44 20 8995 2367

#957
Kimchee To Go
Cuisines: Korean, Fast Food
Average price: £26-45
Area: Bloomsbury
Address: 106 New oxford Street
London WC1A
Phone: +44 20 7637 0937

#958
Pod
Cuisines: Sandwiches
Average price: £11-25
Area: Liverpool Street / Broadgate
Address: 162-163
London Wall London EC2M
5QD **Phone:** +44 20 7256
5506

#959
Nipa
Cuisines: Thai
Average price: £26-45
Area: Bayswater
Address: Lancaster Terrace
London W2 2TY
Phone: +44 20 7551 6039

#960
The Caspian
Cuisines: Persian/Iranian
Average price: £11-25
Area: Lee
Address: 117 Burnt Ash Road
London SE12 8RA
Phone: +44 20 8297 1170

#961
Falafel King
Cuisines: Falafel
Average price: Under £10
Area: Kensal Town
Address: 274 Portobello Road
London W10 5TE
Phone: +44 20 8964 2279

#962
The Montagu
Cuisines: British, Hotel
Average price: £26-45
Area: Marylebone
Address: 30 Portman Square
London W1H 7BH
Phone: +44 20 7299 2037

#963
Reynolds Let's Graze
Cuisines: Sandwiches
Average price: Under £10
Area: Fitzrovia
Address: 34-35 Eastcastle Street
London W1W 8DW
Phone: +44 20 7580 2290

#964
FlatPlanet
Cuisines: Sandwiches, Fast Food
Average price: Under £10
Area: Soho
Address: 39 Great Marlborough Street
London W1F 7JG
Phone: +44 20 7734 3133

#965
Peppers & Spice
Cuisines: Caribbean, Fast Food
Average price: Under £10
Area: De Beauvoir, Newington Green
Address: 40 Balls Pond Rd
London N1 4AU
Phone: +44 20 7275 9818

#966
Sourced Market
Cuisines: Farmers Market, Cafe
Average price: £11-25
Area: King's Cross
Address: Pancras Road
London N1C 4QL
Phone: +44 20 7833 9352

#967
Yipin China Restaurant
Cuisines: Chinese
Average price: £11-25
Area: Angel, Islington
Address: 70-72 Liverpool Road
London N1 0QD
Phone: +44 20 7354 3388

#968
The Ladbroke Arms
Cuisines: Gastropub
Average price: £26-45
Area: Notting Hill
Address: 54 Ladbroke Road
London W11 3NW
Phone: +44 20 7727 6648

#969
Mirch Masala
Cuisines: Indian, Pakistani
Average price: £11-25
Area: Whitechapel
Address: 111-113 Commercial Road
London E1 1RD
Phone: +44 20 7377 0155

#970
The Bishop
Cuisines: Gastropub
Average price: £11-25
Area: East Dulwich
Address: 25 Lordship Lane
London SE22 8EW
Phone: +44 20 8693 3994

#971
Almeida Restaurant
Cuisines: French
Average price: £11-25
Area: Islington
Address: 30 Almeida Street
London N1 1AD
Phone: +44 20 7354 4777

#972
All Star Lanes
Cuisines: Bowling, American
Average price: £26-45
Area: Bayswater
Address: 6 Porchester Gardens
London W2 4DB
Phone: +44 20 7313 8360

#973
Euphorium Bakery
Cuisines: Coffee & Tea, Bakery, Breakfast
& Brunch
Average price: £11-25
Area: Islington
Address: 202 Upper Street
London N1 1RQ
Phone: +44 20 7704 6905

#974
Boundary
Cuisines: French, European, Hotel
Average price: £26-45
Area: Shoreditch
Address: 2-4 Boundary Street
London E2 7DD
Phone: +44 20 7729 1051

#975
Ya Hala
Cuisines: Middle Eastern, Halal
Average price: £11-25
Area: Paddington
Address: 26
London Street
London W2 1HH
Phone: +44 20 7262 1111

#976
Le Pain Quotidien
Cuisines: Breakfast & Brunch,
Tea Room, Belgian
Average price: £11-25
Area: King's Cross
Address: Pancras Road
London NW1 2QP
Phone: +44 20 3657 6946

#977
Charlotte's Place
Cuisines: British
Average price: £11-25
Area: Ealing
Address: 16 St Matthews Road
London W5 3JT
Phone: +44 20 8567 7541

#978
Azou
Cuisines: African, Moroccan
Average price: £11-25
Area: Hammersmith
Address: 375 King Street
London W6 9NJ
Phone: +44 20 8563 7266

#979
Nid Ting
Cuisines: Thai
Average price: £11-25
Area: Holloway Road, Upper Holloway
Address: 533 Holloway Road
London N19 4BT
Phone: +44 20 7263 0506

#980
The Heron
Cuisines: Pub, Thai
Average price: Under £10
Area: Paddington **Address:**
Norfolk Crescent London
W2 2DN
Phone: +44 20 7724 8463

#981
Casa Del Habano
Cuisines: Hotel, Restaurant,
Cocktail Bar
Average price: £11-25
Area: Soho
Address: 100 Wardour Street
London W1F 0TN
Phone: +44 20 7314 4001

#982
Côte
Cuisines: Breakfast & Brunch,
French, Brasserie
Average price: £11-25
Area: Bayswater
Address: 98 Westbourne Grove
London W2 4
Phone: +44 20 7792 3298

#983
Thailand Cuisines:
Thai **Average price:**
£11-25
Area: New Cross
Address: 15 Lewisham Way
London SE14 6PP
Phone: +44 20 8691 4040

#984
Marie's Cafe
Cuisines: Coffee & Tea, Thai
Average price: Under £10
Area: Southwark, Waterloo
Address: 90 Lower Marsh
London SE1 7AB
Phone: +44 20 7928 1050

#985
Chamomile
Cuisines: Coffee & Tea,
Breakfast & Brunch, Cafe
Average price: £11-25
Area: Chalk Farm
Address: 45 England's Lane
London NW3 4YD
Phone: +44 20 7586 4580

#986
Grand Union Camden
Cuisines: Burgers, Pizza, Cocktail Bar
Average price: £11-25
Area: Camden Town
Address: 102-104 Camden Road
London NW1 9EA
Phone: +44 20 7485 4530

#987
Giraffe
Cuisines: British
Average price: £11-25
Area: Victoria
Address: 120 Wilton Rd
London SW1V 1JZ
Phone: +44 20 7233 8303

#988
Bombay Brasserie
Cuisines: Indian
Average price: £26-45
Area: South Kensington
Address: Courtfield Road
London SW7 4QH
Phone: +44 20 7370 4040

#989
The Phoenix
Cuisines: Gastropub
Average price: £11-25
Area: Westminster
Address: 14 Palace Street
London SW1E 5JA
Phone: +44 20 7828 8136

#990
Quaglino's Restaurant
Cuisines: European, Brasserie
Average price: £26-45
Area: St James's
Address: 16 Bury Street
London SW1Y 6AJ
Phone: +44 20 7930 6767

#991
Phoenix Palace
Cuisines: Chinese
Average price: £26-45
Area: Marylebone
Address: 3-5 Glentworth Street
London NW1 5PG
Phone: +44 20 7486 3515

#992
The Albany
Cuisines: Pub, British
Average price: £11-25
Area: Fitzrovia
Address: 240 Great Portland Street
London W1W 5QU
Phone: +44 20 7387 0221

#993
Byron
Cuisines: American, Burgers
Average price: £11-25
Area: Trafalgar Square
Address: 11 Haymarket
London SW1Y 4BP
Phone: +44 20 7925 0276

#994
The Oak
Cuisines: Pizza, Mediterranean
Average price: £11-25
Area: Bayswater, Notting Hill
Address: 137 Westbourne Park Road
London W2 5QL
Phone: +44 20 7221 3355

#995
La Pappardella
Cuisines: Pizza, Italian
Average price: £11-25
Area: Earls Court
Address: 253 Old Brompton Road
London SW5 9HP
Phone: +44 20 7373 7777

#996
Cafe TPT
Cuisines: Coffee & Tea, Chinese
Average price: £11-25
Area: Chinatown
Address: 21 Wardour Street
London W1D 6PN
Phone: +44 20 7734 7980

#997
Admiral Codrington
Cuisines: Pub, British
Average price: £26-45
Area: Chelsea
Address: 17 Mossop Street
London SW3 2LY
Phone: +44 20 7581 0005

#998
Sea Fish
Cuisines: Fish & Chips
Average price: Under £10
Area: Islington
Address: 205 Upper Street
London N1 1RQ
Phone: +44 20 7354 0276

#999
The Peasant
Cuisines: Gastropub
Average price: £11-25
Area: Clerkenwell
Address: 240 St John Street
London EC1V 4PH
Phone: +44 20 7336 7726

#1000
Butlers Wharf Chop House
Cuisines: British
Average price: £26-45
Area: London Bridge, Shad Thames
Address: 36E Shad Thames
London SE1 2YE
Phone: +44 20 7403 3403

Printed in Great Britain
by Amazon